The ROUTINE-BUILDING Handbook

Your All-in-One Habit Builder for Increased Productivity, Inspired Work, and Lasting Success

Ashley Brown

Published by:
Ulysses Press
PO Box 3440
Berkeley, CA 94703
www.ulyssespress.com

ISBN: 978-1-64604-246-3
Library of Congress Control Number: 2021937739

Printed in the United States by Kingery Printing Company
10 9 8 7 6 5 4 3 2 1

Acquisitions editor: Claire Sielaff
Managing editor: Claire Chun
Project editor: Bridget Thoreson
Editor: Renee Rutledge
Proofreader: Barbara Schultz
Front cover design: Ashley Pine
Interior design and layout: what!design @ whatweb.com
Production assistant: Yesenia Garcia-Lopez

To you, the woman who desires more,
may this book be a stepping stone toward
the abundant life you ABSOLUTELY deserve!

CONTENTS

INTRODUCTION

When it comes to routine building, I've noticed there are usually two types of people: those who thoroughly enjoy routines and those who aren't sure if routines can actually work for them. No matter which side you're on, it's important to understand that routines can be an extremely useful tool for managing the chaos and beauty that is life—a springboard that can keep you on track with your highest values. Not only do they help you systematize your actions and lessen decision-making, routines are also an extremely powerful way to add ease and joy to your every day.

I like to compare routines to the silver bar that clicks in place and keeps you safe on a roller coaster. With this silver bar secured, you feel safer on the ride and able to experience maximum joy. Think about it: without the safety bar to hold you in place, you would be more hesitant to get on the ride, anxious about what could happen, and unsure if you would survive. This is very similar to life without routine.

Living life without intentional routines is unpredictable, which can cause discomfort, stress, and anxiety. But with the safety bar of routines to secure you on the ride, there is a freedom and excitement for what's to come, stability when the unexpected twists and turns show up, and the feeling of being grounded and secure no matter what. Of course, this doesn't mean you will never experience hardships, but the safety net of routines helps to lighten your load and make the hard days more tolerable.

It's possible I'm a bit biased because routines have been a positive driving force in my life, and if it were up to me, everyone would see them in the same light as I do—as an intentional way to live your most fulfilling life. Growing up, I was always the girl with a planner in her backpack and colored pens on her desk. I loved anything that kept me organized, from a three-ring binder to multicolored highlighters. I would get bent out of shape about the slightest change in routine. Thankfully I've become much more flexible since then, and although I've learned to go with the flow, I still thrive on routine.

This became crystal clear when I lost my routine during my two-year bout as a stay-at-home mom. After being at home for only a month or two, my life quickly took a turn for the worse, and I began to feel depleted, on edge, and doubtful of the decision to leave my full-time job. My home was messier than it had ever been, I wasn't spending quality time with my daughter like I had imagined, and I quickly lost sight of myself and my mental health. The bright side is this sucky part of my life didn't last too long. With prayer and a strong will to turn things around, I leaned on what had always helped me thrive: routines. With much trial and error, I slowly but surely found my happiness, power, and peace—one routine at a time. I strongly remember cultivating a morning routine that started my day with gratitude practice and a bedtime routine that included reflective journaling and meditation to ease my mind. Funny enough, the bedtime routine is still going strong. When I reflect on that time, I'm in awe. Routines dramatically shifted my life in a positive direction and brought me back to life.

Enough about me. You're here, which means in some sort of way you are ready to adopt routines as your own. Kudos to you. Maybe you want to create that perfect morning routine you hear everyone talking about but haven't quite figured out. Or you're looking to keep up with cleaning because your laundry and kitchen have taken on a mind of their own. You could also be clueless about which routine you need—you just know you need one and you need it now. Lucky for you, you have this book.

Before you dive in, it's important to understand what you're getting yourself into. In order to have the most success with routine building, you must be clear on the purpose and benefits of routines. I describe a routine as an intentional flow of actions done consistently. Simply put, a routine is a consistent set of steps you take to get a specific result. In my experience with routines, I've found them to have three main benefits:

1. The structure and predictability they provide create profound comfort and clarity.

2. Routines decrease stress and reduce mental load through consistent repetition of actions.

3. Lastly, routines help you carry out your core values by directly aligning your actions with what matters most to you.

With these benefits, routines can have an extremely powerful impact on your life, helping you manage your time and energy with ease. They can take you from feeling burned out, overwhelmed, and fragmented to feeling in control, grounded, and overjoyed.

Although routines provide a range of positive benefits, they're frequently rejected and mislabeled. For example, "routine" has become synonymous with words such as "rigid," "restrictive," and "boring." Maybe you have begun to think of routines as stifling to your creativity, lacking in freedom, or too predictable to be fun. If you're a routine rebel, hear me out. Routines can align with your go-with-the-flow style while also adding structure where you need it most. I have found that routine building is less challenging when you understand it can be flexible, offering you the power to create your own guidelines.

Whether you're a routine lover or still hesitant to give routines a shot, to drive the process, you must believe it can be freeing, flexible, and fun. You opened this book for a reason, and I want you to have success. Whether you want smoother mornings, empty laundry baskets, an earlier bedtime for your kids, better health, or more uninterrupted alone time, you're in the right place. Routines will get you there. Commit to the process and watch the magic begin.

How to Use This Book

This handbook is your all-in-one routine builder. It can be used as a practical resource to guide you along the routine-building journey. This book is organized into the following three phases: Notice Your Need, Frame Your Flow, and Protect Your Peace. Each phase is a step in the routine-building process and includes mindset work, practical activities, and answers to commonly asked questions.

If your time is limited, you can use this book to troubleshoot. To find an answer to a specific question, you can start with the applicable FAQ chapters or use the index to direct you to the appropriate page. If you're a mom, be sure to take a peek at the For Mamas section, dedicated solely to helping you overcome challenges faced when creating and maintaining routines as a mom.

Please remember, this book is intended to help you cultivate unique routines to live life with ease and intention. You may have the urge to create routines for every aspect of your life, but don't allow routines to cripple your flexibility.. Routines are meant to create freedom and empowerment through the structure and stability they provide, but there is also beauty and meaning in the unstructured parts of life. When you use routines effectively you have an opportunity to be more present throughout your day and experience the fullness and beauty of life.

Before you begin, think about where you are in the routine-building process. If you are trying to decide which routine to start, begin with phase one. If you are ready to begin creating your ideal routine, start with phase two. If you've been struggling to keep your routine going, phase three can help. Take your time with this book. If you find yourself becoming overwhelmed, you have permission to take a break and start again when the time feels right. Remember, the most successful routines are built with knowledge and patience. I'm so excited for your journey ahead. Dive in. Here's to starting, maintaining, and enjoying routines!

Part 1
NOTICE YOUR NEED
(Assessing Routines)

Chapter 1
START WITH THE END IN MIND

When I first began building intentional routines as a stay-at-home mom, I didn't know what to expect. I stumbled more times than I can count. I would create a routine, start it with high hopes, and find myself back at the drawing board a few weeks later. I thought routine building would be easier since I naturally move toward routine, but this wasn't the case at all. I was confused and ill equipped, but I never gave up. After months of hits and misses, I sat down to assess what was going wrong and to understand why some of my routines were simple to create and maintain while others were not. Over time I discovered what helps to create successful routines: a positive perspective, patience, and a willingness to start again.

Perspective Is Everything

Ever hear the phrase, "your thoughts become your reality"? The truth is, if you choose to view routines with a negative and unrealistic lens, you will inevitably create negative and unrealistic routines. I cautiously avoid words like "daily," "boring," and "restrictive." Routines are what you make them. If you want routines that are enjoyable and easy to maintain, you first have to believe routines can be fun and easy to maintain. Having a positive perspective and clarity of intent will help you find success with routine building.

If routines are boring or restrictive, it's either due to a lack of knowledge or they were created with this intent. Rest assured, if you enjoy going with the flow or consider yourself a spontaneous person, routines can still be your jam. Please don't limit your view of routines. Routines give you the power of choice in the following respects, so choose wisely, my friend:

- **Timing:** You can decide on the time of day you want to do the routine and the length of time you want the routine to be.

- **Frequency:** You can decide how often to do the routine (daily, weekly, or monthly).

- **Place:** You can decide where to do the routine and change this location if and when needed.

- **Actions:** You have ultimate control in deciding the steps of your routine and the actions you will take.

Trial and Error Is Okay

Starting over doesn't feel good, but it can be necessary when building routines. It would be extremely rare for anyone to create a routine and never change it; that's nearly impossible. I wish someone had told me this during my infancy stage of routine building. It would have saved me a bunch of frustration and time. I consider myself a recovering perfectionist, and my journey with routines has taught me some very valuable lessons, including the fact that progress is better than perfection. Even with the help of this book, you are likely to experience trial and error, and that's okay. See it as your compass, pointing you in the right direction. Don't run from it, lean into it. Say it with me, "Trial and error is okay." After all, that's how this book was born.

Don't Rush the Process

I get it, your time is of the essence. With technology delivering information at a rapid pace and instant gratification available at the touch of a button, no wonder our patience is growing slimmer and slimmer. But every journey takes time, and routine building is no different. Impatience with the process can damage your results. Ever rush to cook dinner and regret doing so because it tasted like crap? Try rushing to build your routine—it'll taste like crap too. I understand if your life is in desperate need of routine. Maybe your kids are driving you nuts, your mental health is taking a turn, or your physical health is in jeopardy. Rushing the process by throwing spaghetti at the wall won't help; thoughtfully creating the right plan will.

Your Easy Yes

Along with knowing what to expect when building a routine, it can be equally important to have an anchor, or a strong motivating factor, to keep you on track. You'll learn more about motivation in Part 3, but essentially, a proven way to stay motivated is to keep your end goal in mind. This is what I like to call your "easy yes." Your easy yes will help you get out of bed at 4:30 in the morning, even when everyone else is sleeping comfortably in bed. It'll push you to jog in the rain knowing you just washed your hair. Your easy yes will catapult you to clean the kitchen when the kids go to bed, although you would rather turn on Netflix.

Your easy yes is the main reason you say yes to including routine in your life. It must be heartfelt, personal, meaningful, and strong enough to drive you to take action immediately. You can think of it this way: What overarching goal do you want to accomplish by building routines? For example, my easy yes is to live my fullest life with ease, joy, and intention. I believe routines help me achieve this goal while keeping me focused and motivated. For example, my morning routine allows me to ease into my day and live it with intention. I'm a 9 a.m. morning, person, which means my brain doesn't wake up until then. My morning routine includes a simple body massage, prayer, and mental stimulation, which usually consists of picking up my phone and reading a scripture from my favorite Bible app.

Remember, your easy yes is personal. You don't have to broadcast it to the world. It doesn't have to be a profound statement that moves you to tears. Your easy yes can be a series of words describing how you want your life to feel. It can also be a short affirmation of intention. It's your choice, and the sky's the limit. To provide context, below are a few examples of easy yeses from women using routines to improve their lives. Take time to think of your easy yes because it will become your anchor. Here are some easy yes examples:

- Be more productive.
- Keep my home peaceful and relaxing.
- Spend time being present with my family.
- Focus on my higher goals.
- Keep a clear head.
- Avoid procrastination.
- Be a better mom.
- Stay structured and grounded.
- Manage stress.
- Spend mommy alone time.
- Ease stress and hold myself accountable.

How to Determine Your Easy Yes

Use the lines provided here or take out a journal or blank sheet of paper (at the top of the paper, write the words "My Easy Yes"). Journal for an entire ten minutes by answering these questions:

- What will routines help me experience and achieve in my life?
- What would make routines an easy yes for me?

My Easy Yes

Routine Wisdom: Your First Yes
May Not Be Your Easy Yes

Almost eight months after giving birth to my second child, I was excited to start an exercise routine to decrease the size of my belly. I wanted to start my journey toward a six-pack of abs and, honestly, I would have been a happy mama if my separated abdominal muscles, a medical condition called "diastasis recti," would come together.

At that time, I considered getting rid of my kangaroo pouch as my easy yes. But after a month of inconsistent exercise, I realized my easy yes wasn't enough to keep me motivated. I was constantly choosing TV over exercise, and I found myself making the excuse that I needed more time. After months passed, I committed to exercising at least three days a week. After the first week of exercising, I realized exercise was a form of self-care that strengthened my mindset and increased my energy. A strong mindset and increased energy became my easy yes and helped me crush a thirty-day exercise routine. Moral of the story? Your first yes may not be your easy yes. Sometimes you have to dig deeper.

As you begin building routines, remember there are no hard-and-fast rules. Your routine will serve you best when you keep a positive perspective, get comfortable with trial and error, and trust the process. Start by determining your easy yes. This will become your anchor during the journey and will put you back on course when challenges arise. Beginning with the end in mind is a major key to your success.

Chapter 2
CHOOSING THE RIGHT ROUTINE

When my life was in shambles as a stay-at-home mom, the first routine I started was a morning routine. Not too surprising, right? It seems everyone wants a great morning routine, but let me tell you why I chose to start with this one. I needed to find myself again. I viewed my morning routine as self-care because I was able to focus solely on myself without distractions and before the daily needs of my family began. I knew that in order to rediscover who I was, I needed to care for myself constantly, and my morning routine provided this opportunity. Making the decision to bypass starting a laundry routine or kitchen routine was an easy choice. I knew in order to give to my home fully, I had to give to myself first. Choosing to create a self-care routine to put myself first was a no-brainer. If choosing which routine to start isn't as easy, rest assured, there are ways to make decision-making a simple process.

Improving Your Current Routines

Whether you realize it or not, you currently have routines. You do the laundry regularly, have a flow to your morning, and clean the kitchen in a particular way. Decision-making starts with examining the indications for a new routine. Let's dive into three major indications that an improved routine is needed.

1. Something is missing. The routine lacks a certain action that could make the process smoother or more efficient.

2. The routine is outdated. You continue to do the same routine although it doesn't feel in alignment with your current lifestyle.

3. It could be better. When doing the routine, you wish there was a simpler way of going about it.

It's easy to stay stuck doing things that aren't conducive to managing your life with ease. We all have learned to care for our home, ourselves, and our loved ones in a specific way but sometimes fail to examine if what we have learned is creating a positive outcome for our life. My mom would kill me if she knew I washed my clothing and towels together rather than separate, like she taught me. If I hadn't been brave enough to question how I wash laundry, I would have stayed stressed doing it her way. I made the choice to change the process, and now I feel much lighter without the extra load of laundry weighing me down.

Determining which routine to create and start can be daunting. The most common routines you can create include morning, exercise, and skin care routines, but the list is pretty endless. It can be overwhelming to decide which part of your life gets priority when many parts need improving. In my routine-building experience, I've noticed that the following three trends can cause poor decision-making:

- Making decisions in stress mode
- Constant comparison
- Lack of clarity (being unconscious of what is important to you or unsure of which routine will help you as an individual)

Let's talk about making decisions in stress mode. It hardly ever works out. I made this mistake during a very chaotic season of my life. My home was falling apart, and the only thing I could think to do was plan. This may sound like a smart choice, but it led to more stress. At the time, planning looked like writing down everything in my head on a sheet of paper. Seeing the long list of things I needed to do brought about a lot of anxiety, and the overwhelm led to my accomplishing little. Moral of the story: I didn't need a plan, I first needed to decompress and clear my head.

Next up is comparison. I remember speaking with a burned-out mom who struggled with deciding whether to start a laundry routine or a bedtime routine for her kids. She explained how she felt like a bad mom because her friend with the same amount of kids seemed to "have things together." Her friend never complained about the laundry and her kids went to bed without a fuss. After our conversation, she realized she had been comparing her life to her friend's life As we continued to talk through her routines, she began to recognize she did have a decent laundry and bedtime routine; however, her lack of self-care was her biggest issue. She needed to focus on caring for herself because her sanity and peace were of utmost importance to her, and she wanted to value this decision. The insight she gained by avoiding comparison and honoring what she truly needed led her to choose the right routine for her life.

The last culprit to dampen decision-making is a lack of clarity. This can look like stalled progress or failing to answer the question, "Which routine do I need most right now?" It's no coincidence that hundreds of women have taken my free routine assessment to get help with answering this question. The number one problem I've witnessed doing this work is being unclear about which routine will best support one's life. This usually stems from perfectionism and overthinking the decision. Like myself, if you struggle with a perfectionist mindset, remember, choosing which routine to start doesn't need to be a perfect decision.

I see it all the time. We are knee-deep in stress, too concerned with what others are doing instead of focusing on our own actions, and unsure of what we need, which leads us to doing way too much, all at once. It's time to break these unhealthy cycles. Here are three ways to do so.

1. Overcome the Overwhelm

Working as a bedside nurse taught me a life-changing lesson: you can't think clearly when you're stressed. Ever burn your meal while cooking because your kids were screaming in the background? Or frantically look for your lost keys, only to find them when you stop looking? It makes sense. Making decisions when you're overwhelmed hardly pays off. Before trying to decide which routine you need most right now, reduce your stress. Clear your head of all the junk that's roaming around, clouding your judgement and causing you anxiety. Once your head is in a better mental space, you'll be ready to make better decisions.

Reduce Stress

Try the following stress-reducing activities:

- **4-4-8 Breathing:** Inhale for 4 counts, hold for 4 counts, exhale for 8 counts.

- **Brain Dumping:** On the lines below or a blank sheet of paper, write down everything you are currently thinking of. It doesn't have to make sense, just write.

....

....

....

....

....

- **Dance Party:** Turn on your favorite song or music playlist, and move your body..

2. Kill the Comparison

I get it. It can be hard not to compare yourself to others. You see your neighbor out for a run at 8 p.m. and begin to wonder why you just started the fourth episode of *This Is Us*. Comparison can be inspirational, but it can also be triggering and lead to decisions outside your best interest. If you compare yourself to the neighbor running after a long day, you may instantly think you need to take up running instead of continuing to go to your virtual Zumba classes three days a week. You can quickly forget how your exercise routine is fun and works with your schedule. Remember to do what works for you, no matter what anyone else says or thinks. Comparison is a distraction, and there's no room for distraction when building routines.

Routine Wisdom: Your Routine, Your Rhythm

We are all routine oriented, but our routines may manifest in different ways. For example, Michelle may like to do the same exercise every morning while Hannah prefers to randomly choose her exercise every morning. They are both in routine and have the same outcome, but their steps to achieving their goal caters to who they are as individuals.

3. Keep the Commitment

This isn't the time to showcase your multitasking skills. Create one routine at a time, and you are far more likely to have success when committing to and maintaining it. However, this can be easy to forget if you are flooded with the excitement of starting a new routine or unclear on which part of your life is most likely to benefit from improvement. Please understand that building multiple routines and starting them all at once won't save you time or lead to quicker results. Instead, the opposite outcome ensues: more time spent and stalled progress.

When you stay committed to building one routine, you're committing to a better outcome. Plus, by committing to one routine and finding success in it, you gain proof that the process works and confidence within yourself, which gives you momentum to move on to the next routine with a positive, optimistic attitude. Once you commit to one routine at a time, the question becomes, which one?

Step 1: Determine Which Routines Work for You

It's easy to focus on what's not working versus what's going well. This can cause overwhelm and the tendency to compare. By paying attention to which routines are actually working in your life, you'll lessen the possibility of getting stuck on the hamster wheel of stress and confusion. This will stop you from exploring unnecessary routines and allow you to connect with the joy and positivity within your current routines. With this positive outlook, you're likely to find the motivation you need to create a new or improved routine with clarity, intention, and focus. You'll be able to clearly determine the routines greatly supporting your life and better identify the routines most important to adopt in this current season. To determine if your routine is working well for your life, ask yourself the following questions.

- Does it make my life easier to manage?

....

....

....

....

....

- Is it tolerable and simple to maintain?

....

....

....

....

....

- Does it lessen my load (physical, mental, emotional) in this season of life?

....

....

....

....

....

- Does it help me remain intentional and proactive?

....

....

....

....

....

Step 2: Do a Gut Check and/or Complete a Routine Assessment

Your intuition is powerful and instinctively knows what you need. When deciding which routine to start, do a simple gut check. This can look like asking yourself what you need most right now and trusting the first thing that comes to mind. It can look like you getting still and examining which area of your home and life has been causing you immense frustration and/or anxiety. Trust that your intuition knows what's best, and follow it.

If you're not quite sold on allowing your intuition to lead your decision-making and would rather have information to guide your decision, completing a routine assessment is another option. A routine assessment is a simple process of examining your current routines in order to determine which to improve first. However, this can be a daunting task if you believe you don't have any routines to assess or you're unsure of where to start. For the sake of simplifying this process, consider the following five routine categories:

Routine Categories

Routines don't fit into a box and can vary dramatically from person to person and family to family. Below are five routine categories to take into consideration and a few examples to showcase how versatile routines can be. This is by no means an exhaustive list, but rather a selection of examples to inspire your creativity as you work to build your own unique routines.

Cooking

This category includes the actions you take in order to feed yourself and/or your family. From planning to preparing your meals, think about your daily and weekly actions associated with cooking and nutrition. You may consider building a cooking routine if you want to eat out less, save money, consume fewer processed foods, or enjoy a phone-free sit-down meal with the family. Here are some examples of cooking routines.

⇨ **Meal-Planning Routine #1**
Suggested steps: Choose meals > Make grocery list > Go grocery shopping
Frequency: Weekly
Timing: ~ 2 hours

⇨ Meal-Planning Routine #2

Suggested steps: Decide weekly meals > Make grocery list > Place grocery delivery order

Frequency: Weekly

Timing: ~ 2 to 3 hours (depending on how quick the delivery is)

⇨ Meal-Prep Routine #1

Suggested steps: Cook two veggies > Cook two carbohydrates > Cook two proteins

Frequency: Weekly

Timing: ~ 2 hours

⇨ Meal-Prep Routine #2

Suggested steps: Precut veggies > Pre-season protein

Frequency: Weekly

Timing: ~ 30 minutes

⇨ Family Dinner Routine

Suggested steps: Cook dinner > Set table > Eat as family

Frequency: Each evening (at-home meals)

Timing: ~ 2 hours

⇨ Dinner Table Routine

Suggested steps: Turn off phones > Pray > Eat

Frequency: Each evening with family meals

Timing: ~ 1 hour

Here are some blank templates you can use to identify cooking routines in your life:

⇨ .... Routine

Steps:...

....

Frequency:...

Timing:..

⇨ .... Routine

Steps:...

....

Frequency:...

Timing:..

⇨ .... Routine

Steps:...

....

Frequency:...

Timing:..

⇨ .... Routine

Steps:...

....

Frequency:...

Timing:..

Cleaning

This category includes actions to clean and organize your home. This can be daily cleaning tasks or weekly cleaning tasks. A clean home leads to more clarity and calm. Cleaning routines such as laundry or kitchen routines can help prevent massive buildup and keep cleaning your home manageable. Some examples are:

⇨ **Laundry Routine**

Suggested steps: Wash load in a.m. > Fold and put away in p.m.

Frequency: Daily

Timing: ~ 2 hours

⇨ **Kitchen Routine #1**

Suggested steps: Unload dishwasher > Load and start dishwasher > Sweep floor

Frequency: Daily

Timing: ~ 1 hour

⇨ **Kitchen Routine #2**

Suggested steps: Wash dishes > Clean countertops > Sweep floor

Frequency: Daily

Timing: ~ 1 hour

⇨ **Tidy Routine #1**

Suggested Steps: Clear floors > Wipe countertops > Put items back where they belong

Frequency: Daily

Timing: ~ 20 minutes

⇨ **Tidy Routine #2**

Suggested Steps: Clear floors > Sweep/vacuum floor > Organize items

Frequency: Daily

Timing: ~ 30 minutes

⇨ **Home Refresh Routine**

Suggested Steps: Clean bathrooms > Sweep/vacuum floors > Tidy bedrooms > Empty trash

Frequency: Weekly

Timing: ~ 2 hours

Here are some blank templates you can use to identify cleaning routines in your life:

⇨ .... **Routine**

Steps:..

....

Frequency:..

Timing:...

⇨ .... **Routine**

Steps:..

....

Frequency:..

Timing:...

⇨ .... **Routine**

Steps:..

....

Frequency:..

Timing:..

⇨ .... **Routine**

Steps:..

....

Frequency:..

Timing:..

Children

The children category includes activities that make up your child's day, from morning to bedtime. This can include activities you do with your kids, activities they do with others, or activities they do alone. When children know what to expect it makes them feel safe and secure. Creating routines for your kids can help you achieve goals such as less screen time, independent play, more physical activity, or uninterrupted one-on-one time. Consider these routines:

⇨ **Morning Routine #1**

Suggested steps: Use restroom > Brush teeth > Wash face > Get dressed

Frequency: Daily

Timing: ~ 15 minutes

⇨ Morning Routine #2

Suggested steps: Wash face > Brush teeth > Put on clothes > Read book

Frequency: Daily

Timing: ~ 25 minutes

⇨ Bedtime Routine #1

Suggested steps: Bath time > Read book > Prayer

Frequency: Daily

Timing: ~ 45 minutes

⇨ Bedtime Routine #2

Suggested steps: Put on PJs > Talk about the day > Lights out

Frequency: Daily

Timing: ~ 20 minutes

⇨ Homeschool Routine

Suggested steps: Learning > Play > Lunch > Nap > Snack

Frequency: 5 days a week

Timing: ~ 6 hours

⇨ Midday Routine

Suggested Steps: Play/Learn > Lunch > Nap > Snack > TV time

Frequency: Daily

Timing: ~ 6 hours

Here are some blank templates you can use to identify routines involving children in your life:

➡ .... Routine

Steps: ....

....

Frequency: ....

Timing: ....

➡ .... Routine

Steps: ....

....

Frequency: ....

Timing: ....

➡ .... Routine

Steps: ....

....

Frequency: ....

Timing: ....

➡ .... Routine

Steps: ....

....

Frequency: ....

Timing: ....

Self-Care

The self-care category involves the numerous ways in which you care for yourself, whether physically, mentally, emotionally, or spiritually. Establishing a self-care routine can help you stay on track with your personal or professional goals and prevent you from losing sight of your wants and needs. Consider starting a self-care routine if you are a caregiver, have a high-demand career, or are under tremendous stress. Examples are:

⇨ **Morning Routine #1**

Suggested steps: Meditation > Movement

Frequency: Daily

Timing: ~ 45 minutes

⇨ **Morning Routine #2**

Suggested steps: Shower > Skin care > Plan day

Frequency: Daily

Timing: ~ 1 hour

⇨ **Evening Routine**

Suggested steps: Snack > Watch TV > Plan next day

Frequency: Daily

Timing: ~ 1.5 hours

⇨ **Bedtime Routine**

Suggested steps: Shower > Journal > Read

Frequency: Daily

Timing: ~ 1.5 hours

⇨ Rest Routine #1

Suggested steps: Get still > Deep breaths > Sit in silence for 10 minutes

Frequency: Daily

Timing: ~ 15 minutes

⇨ Rest Routine #2

Suggested steps: Sit down > Watch TV show

Frequency: Daily after work

Timing: ~1 hour

⇨ Exercise Routine

Suggested steps: Get dressed > Drink glass of water > Exercise > Drink water

Frequency: 3 to 4 days a week

Timing: ~ 1 hour

Here are some blank templates you can use to identify self-care routines in your life:

⇨ .... Routine

Steps: ....

....

Frequency: ....

Timing: ....

⇨ .... **Routine**

Steps:..

....

Frequency:..

Timing:...

⇨ .... **Routine**

Steps:..

....

Frequency:..

Timing:...

⇨ .... **Routine**

Steps:..

....

Frequency:..

Timing:...

Planning

This category includes any sort of planning activities and preparation for work, school, or travel. A planning routine will help you stay proactive and intentional. You may find a planning routine useful if you are constantly forgetting things, have an overactive mind, need to keep track of current tasks and projects, or like checking off boxes. Examples are:

⇨ Weekly Planning Routine

Suggested steps: Brain dump > Decide top three priorities > Schedule weekly to-dos

Frequency: Weekly

Timing: ~ 30 minutes

⇨ Daily Planning Routine

Suggested steps: Preview day > Schedule priorities > Schedule daily desires

Frequency: Daily

Timing: ~ 20 minutes

⇨ Monthly Family-Planning Routine

Suggested steps: Make snack plate > Review everyone's monthly activities/appointments > Schedule all events on calendar

Frequency: Monthly

Timing: ~ 2 hours

⇨ Travel Prep Routine

Suggested steps: Take inventory of what's needed > Address needs > Double-check needs were met

Frequency: Before any trip/vacation

Timing: Depends on what's needed

⇨ Before-Work Routine

Suggested steps: Eat breakfast > Prep lunch bag > Double-check work bag

Frequency: On work days (morning)

Timing: ~ 25 minutes

Here are some blank templates you can use to identify planning routines in your life:

⇨ .... Routine

Steps:...

....

Frequency:..

Timing:...

⇨ .... Routine

Steps:...

....

Frequency:..

Timing:...

⇨ .... Routine

Steps:...

....

Frequency:..

Timing:...

⇨ .... Routine

Steps:...

....

Frequency:..

Timing:...

Now that you have an understanding of each category, you can begin to assess where you can make improvements. To guide your assessments, the series of questions below give you the opportunity to acknowledge which routines are not serving your life so you can begin to create a plan of action.

Routine Assessment Activity

Using the lines here or a blank sheet of paper, write down the name of every routine category you will assess, using a different row for each category. Assess each category with the following three questions, writing "yes" or "no" next to the routine category.

Question 1: Does this routine constantly cause you anxiety or frustration?

Question 2: Do you often overlook or skip this routine?

Question 3: Do you believe improving this routine would create ease in your life?

Routine Category	question 1	question 2	question 3

Look at your responses. If you answered "yes" two or more times within any given category, this indicates your routine needs improvement.

Once you have identified which routines need refining, it's time to commit to working on only one routine category. Focusing on one will make the routine-building process simpler and more manageable. If you're struggling to decide which routine category to focus on, I suggest starting with the simplest routine to get up and going, or this could be the perfect time to do a gut check (see page 29).

Step 3: Choose Your Focus

Once you have chosen the routine category to focus your attention on, it's best for you to select a specific routine within your chosen category. Doing so will give you the clarity and confidence needed to create and maintain the routine. There are a plethora of routines you can create within each category, but only choose one to start with. For example, which specific part of your cleaning routine are you struggling with? Which specific routine do you want to cultivate as a way to care for yourself? Where exactly in your child's day do they need more structure? Details matter when you are routine building. The more niche your routine, the smoother the process.

In the Routine Chart on the following page, you'll notice the five routine categories and specific routines associated with each (see sample routines starting on page 30). This is by no means a complete list but rather some examples I believe are useful. Feel free to adjust or add to the list as needed. If you don't see a routine listed that you want to start, get creative and title your own routine.

For example, I had never heard of a rest routine before creating my own, and now it has become a huge part of my self-care. Remember, you make the rules for your routines.

Routine Chart

Cooking	Cleaning	Children	Self-Care	Planning
Dinner Routine	Laundry Routine	Morning Routine	Exercise Routine	Daily Planning Routine
Meal-Prep Routine	Kitchen Routine	Bedtime Routine	Morning Routine	Weekly Planning Routine
Meal-Planning Routine	Tidy Routine	Learning Routine	Evening Routine	Monthly Planning Routine
Grocery-Shopping Routine	Organizing Routine	Naptime Routine	Bedtime Routine	Children Planning Routine
Recipe-Finding Routine	Mopping Routine	Lunch Routine	Skin Care Routine	Travel-Planning Routine
	Bathroom Routine			

Problem: Rebecca was overwhelmed with the transition to stay-at-home mom. She felt disorganized and hadn't found a solution that could help her organize her day-to-day.

What helped: Rebecca started a planning routine that included breaking down her weekly tasks into categories (cooking, cleaning, children, self-care) and sticking to five or fewer tasks per day.

Outcome: This simple planning routine helped her see planning as less overwhelming and contributed to more clarity and focus. She was able to organize her days as a stay-at-home mom, which brought about peace of mind for Rebecca.

"When I decided to stay home full time, I felt lost and overwhelmed by the disorganization of my day and home. I felt very defeated, angry, and anxious each day. It wasn't until I started reaching out to find mom support systems online that I found Ashley and Routine and Things. Learning about how to establish routines and plan my week more effectively really changed how I feel about myself, my day, and my home. Now I love planning my week and I rely on my routines to carry me through each day, especially the harder days. I never thought to plan my week being a stay-at-home mom, but it has made all the difference. A planning routine is peace for me, and I love how it relaxes my mind and gives me things to look forward to each day and week."

As you may have discovered, choosing the right routine takes time, especially if you want a successful start. It takes intentionality, insight, and trust. Before moving forward, keep these things in mind: de-stress first, avoid comparing yourself to others, and gain the clarity needed to commit to one routine at a time. If you find yourself struggling to decide which routine to start, simply do a gut check, take a quick routine assessment, or do a combination of both. Once you are 95 percent sure which routine you want to start, next up is creating your ideal routine.

Still have questions? Check out the FAQs in Chapter 3.

Chapter 3
ROUTINE ASSESSMENT FAQS

Assessing your routines is about understanding where you currently are in order to move in a direction that best supports your life. This chapter is to help you get unstuck and gain clarity as you decide which routine is right for you. Below are answers to the most frequently asked questions that come up when embarking upon building a new routine.

Q: How do routines really help me?

A: Routines have a range of positive benefits. For example, routines can help you achieve value-based outcomes. With a routine you can align your actions with what you value the most. Let's say you value a healthy lifestyle. You can build a routine that allows you to focus on your health and well-being. Routines can also help you to feel less stress, more intentional, and better able to manage decision fatigue. For example, a meal-planning routine that includes taking an inventory of what you have, creating a list of weekly meals, and grocery shopping will lighten your mental load and lessen frustration at dinner time. I love to describe routines as your warm, cozy blanket when you feel cold. When you have your blanket [routines], you feel comfortable and more likely to enjoy your experience. When the blanket [routines] is removed, you can begin to feel uncomfortable and anxious, which can lead to stress. Having healthy routines in your life can increase your happiness and promote a sense of comfort and well-being.

Q: Are routines the same as habits? What's the difference?

A: Routines are similar to habits, but they are not the same. A habit is a behavior that takes little to no conscious thought, whereas a routine is a repeated series of steps done frequently. A routine can definitely become habitual with constant repetition but requires time and effort to do so. A habit I now have that started as a routine is my skin care. I automatically care for my skin after showering. The steps are on autopilot and keep my skin glowing. Luckily, being great at forming habits is not a requirement for being great at consistently engaging with your routines.

Q: How can I make routine building simple and stress free?

A: Routine building can be simple and stress free after you first understand that it takes time and requires patience. This is extremely helpful to remember when creating routines. If you rush the routine-building process and move without intention, you can sabotage your progress. Take the considerations in this book into account when building any routine, and you will invite simplicity and ease into the process. Chapter 1 is a great place to start if you're looking for a fun and enjoyable way to start building your own routine.

Q: I'm in need of a routine now. From start to finish, how long does it take to build a routine?

A: The time it takes to build a routine will vary from person to person. A contributing factor includes clarity of focus. Do you know which routine you wish to focus on? Another influencing factor is how quickly you make decisions. Finally, the details of your routine can also impact the length of time it takes to create a routine. I have created routines within a few hours, over the course of one day, and across multiple days. If you need a specific routine as soon as possible, you can make it happen as long as you don't compromise your intention throughout the process.

Q: What are signs I may be in need of a routine?

A: Three major signs can indicate that a routine could be beneficial for your life.

1. You have recently experienced a life transition. This could be moving into a new home, having a baby, changing jobs, adopting a new role in the home, starting a new business, sending children to school, experiencing an increase in family size, or undergoing self-growth.

2. Life or home feels off balance or chaotic. When life or home begins to feel unmanageable and stressful, this can be a huge indication you're in need of a new routine or may need to revamp your current routine. I remember constantly feeling burned out, anxious, and annoyed when caring for my home and family. For me, these signs were indicators that I was in need of new routines, specifically self-care and cleaning routines. Luckily, if you're feeling this way, routines can help to add more order and peace to your home and life.

3. You set a new goal. Routines can greatly help you accomplish any goal you have. When you put in place a series of steps that will move you toward your goal, you are more likely to reach success. For example, you may have a goal of caring for yourself more. You can build a self-care routine to repeatedly accomplish this goal. When a new goal arises, instead of tackling the goal head first, pause and think, "Can a routine help me be more efficient and effective as I work to meet my goal's expected outcome?"

Q: Routines aren't my thing, can they still work for me?

A: Without a doubt! Routines work for anyone. If you consider yourself a routine rebel or spontaneous person who loves to go with the flow, routines can still be your jam. Contrary to popular belief, routines do not have to be rigid actions that keep you boxed in. They can include flexibility and contribute to a significant amount of freedom. As an example, my exercise routine includes stretching, movement, and cool down. "Movement" allows for a lot of wiggle room. One day I can decide to practice yoga and the next day I can go for a walk. If the word "routine" makes you uncomfortable, instead of focusing on the word, try shifting your perspective to the outcome routines provide, including increase in time, decrease in stress, and more enjoyment in life.

Q: I'm in need of multiple routines. Is it okay to build them all at once?

A: My motto is "one routine at a time." Building multiple routines at once can get confusing and possibly become overwhelming. To decrease becoming stressed and anxious in creating and maintaining your routines, it's best to focus your attention on one routine only. Once you have a grasp of your new routine, you can begin to build a new one.

Q: What are some ways to easily assess my current routine?

A: You can assess your current routine in two ways:

1. Write out your current routine. It is easier to notice what's is or isn't working in your routine by seeing it visually. Write out your routine step by step below or on a sheet of paper. For each step, consider if the action is necessary, intentional, and timely. Assessing each step of your routine is a great way to make changes and adjust if needed.

Current Routine

Step 1:   O Necessary   O Intentional   O Timely

....

....

Step 2:   O Necessary   O Intentional   O Timely

....

....

Step 3:   O Necessary   O Intentional   O Timely

....

....

Step 4:   O Necessary   O Intentional   O Timely

....

....

Step 5:   O Necessary   O Intentional   O Timely

....

....

2. Take a routine assessment. Taking a detailed inventory of your routines can direct you to needed improvement. You may feel that all of your routines need improvement, which could be possible, but how can you know for sure? Reviewing your routine based on specific criteria gives you the data you need to make an informed decision. To complete a simple routine assessment activity, refer to page 43.

Q: Are there any specific routines that may be helpful for me to consider starting?

A: This will totally depend on your specific needs, but I can share the routines that were personally helpful for me. The routines that presently keep me grounded, at ease, happy, and in alignment with my values are my bedtime routine (for both myself and my children), kitchen routine, tidy routine, and planning routine. These routines keep me sane. My routines give me the freedom to thrive despite the inevitable changes of life. Consider which routine will help you thrive in life and start there.

Q: I can't decide which routine to start. What can help?

A: If you're struggling to choose which routine to build, you can do a gut check or do the routine assessment activity on page 43. Either of these options will help steer you in the right direction. If you still find it challenging to make a choice, I recommend starting with the simplest routine to get up and going. If you're deciding between a few routines, it can be helpful to think about which routine has the least barrier of entry. For example, if you are stuck between a children's routine and a planning routine, I suggest starting with the planning routine because you have more control over planning than you have over your children's response and their adjustment to a new routine. If you are still unsure, simply choose a routine and stick with it. Try not to get hung up on choosing the perfect routine. The most important thing is to start a routine so you can begin to experience more order and peace of mind in your life.

Q: I want my family to be involved, how do I get them on board with routine building?

A: It can be really nice to have your family involved in the routines you create. This will help to lighten your load and create stronger relationships through teamwork. Whether this includes your partner, children, or other family members, communication about why this routine is important and how the routine will help everyone involved is key. Also, involving your family in the routine-building process can be extremely beneficial because it makes them feel more invested in the outcome. There are several other options to get your family on board, including ongoing collaboration, role modeling behavior, and managing expectations. To hear the remainder, check out episode 030 of the *Routine and Things* podcast, located in the resource section of this book.

Part 2
FRAME YOUR FLOW
(Creating Routines)

Chapter 4
LEARNING TO LEAN IN

During my transition from working mom to stay-at-home mom, I struggled greatly. I was constantly behind on cleaning, my daughter was parked in front of the TV, and time for myself was nonexistent. I remember one day in particular. My husband walked through the door after getting off from work and asked me a very simple question, for which I had no response: Did you do anything around the house today? At that moment, I broke out in tears trying to retrace my steps. I had done little for our home that day, and it showed. The dishes were still in the sink from the night before, my daughter was still in her pajamas, and three baskets of laundry were still waiting to be washed. I felt like a horrible partner and mom.

During this season of life, many times I questioned if I made the right decision to be a stay-at-home mom to my daughter. I even regretted it at times. Not many people speak about how your identity shifts when you give up a career to raise a family. I had begun to believe being a steward of my home was not an identity I wanted to claim. I wanted things to go back to how they were when I could successfully manage my life. I tried hard to fit my old routines into my current lifestyle. I would still try to get laundry done on the weekends although I was exhausted from a long week with my daughter and the routine of getting uninterrupted work time during the day was not working. The more I forced them to fit, the more I remained overwhelmed, agitated, and anxious.

After months of feeling stressed and stuck, the pressure became unbearable. That's when I realized my actions were creating an unwanted reality. By controlling every aspect of my life, I was resisting the change my life desperately needed. I saw my situation through a negative lens and failed to recognize the positive benefits of being a stay-at-home mom. It wasn't until I decided to focus on the positive and surrender to the opportunity to care for our home with gratitude and intention that I found some relief. I slowly began to accept that this was where I was meant to be. With acceptance, I felt less overwhelmed and a greater sense of ease and confidence with cultivating routines for my home and life.

Getting to a place where you can fully accept the season you are currently in greatly impacts your routines. The routines you create will better meet the needs of your current lifestyle and you'll be more likely to experience satisfaction in life. If you are currently struggling to accept your current situation or season, I want you to know you're not alone. It can feel scary and uncomfortable to trust and accept life as it is, especially when your current circumstance doesn't feel good. It's important to understand leaning in doesn't mean ignoring or dismissing your experience, but acknowledging the challenges and choosing to sit with the discomfort while also recognizing the positive. Owning the season you're in will unlock the door to so many possibilities for your routines and make the creation process much more enjoyable and successful.

Are You Leaning In?

Accepting how your life looks and feels at any given moment may not always be easy for you. Sometimes we can reject our current situation and not realize it. When I first became a stay-at-home mom, I didn't understand that by wanting my life to resemble my past working lifestyle, I was causing more harm than good. It took me a while to notice how holding on to the past and wanting to escape the present was negatively affecting my life.

Sometimes we can unknowingly hold ourselves back from experiencing joy in the now. Maybe you've been stuck in a cycle of misery because you are afraid to let go of what was or you're too focused on where you want to be a year from now. To help you avoid making the same mistake I did, below is a list of signs that you could be rejecting your current season of life. These signs can help you recognize it may be time to lean in.

- You are constantly comparing your old lifestyle to your current situation.
- You speak more about the past than the present.
- Your old routines still exist, but they don't fit your current lifestyle.
- You want this part of your life to be over.

- You're making progress, but it doesn't feel fast enough for you.

- Your mind is always a few years into the future.

- You refuse to give up routines that no longer serve you or your current life.

- You are unable to see the good in your current situation.

- You make statements that begin with "I wish" or "If only."

- You struggle to remain in the present moment.

If any of these resonates with you, it's okay and totally normal. We all experience moments and have aspects of our lives that we wish were different. It's part of the human experience. Try not to focus on what's wrong in your current season of life. Instead, recognize how this unwanted experience can help you cultivate supportive routines. There's always good in the midst of the bad if you allow yourself to see it. Hold on to this perspective because it can open your heart and allow you to experience abundance within your life. This will, in turn, free you of constant stress and struggle.

I will share what can help you lean into the life that's right in front of you and learn not only to accept it, but also to find purpose and joy in it. Before we get there, it's important to recognize how seasons of life change and to identify which season you're actually in.

Seasons Change: Which One Are You In?

Knowing which season of life you're currently in is imperative to creating routines to meet your specific needs. Understanding your situation isn't about judgment but making necessary improvements. A routine should meet you where you are and propel you to where you want to be. Many of us typically fall into one of the three seasons described below.

Season 1: Life's Good

If you're experiencing this season, you are feeling pretty good in life. You have a handle on things at home, life feels manageable, and you are satisfied with where your life is headed. You more than likely have daily and weekly routines in place that are helping you manage your time and energy. In this season, you may be looking to improve your current routines or add on another routine. In this season, it can be helpful to think about adopting routines that spark creativity, bring about a new hobby, or encourage rest.

Season 2: Life's Getting off Track

In this season, life is starting to feel uncomfortable. You can feel something is off but you're not quite sure what is causing the friction. You have some routines that work and some that need improvement. You may feel your time is not well spent, or there is not enough time in your day to complete what you need to. Things at home are becoming unmanageable, and feelings of stress are starting to creep in. To help in this season, start a routine that focuses on managing your day-to-day tasks to decrease your stress and increase your productivity.

Season 3: Life's a Mess

This is the season when you feel out of control. Your day-to-day feels unorganized, and you wish there was more order. You may be experiencing overwhelm, anxiety, or burnout. The routines you have are no longer working, and it shows greatly. Your home may feel chaotic, and your actions stem from survival mode rather than from intention. In this season, it is common to feel frustrated and unsure of how to get back on track. If you find yourself in this season, start a routine that is centered around you. The renewed confidence restored by self-care will give you the evidence you need to begin to improve your life.

No matter which season you're in, I want you to know you are not alone. Your circumstance does not define who you are; in fact, you are separate from your circumstances. With this clarity in mind you can be empowered to cultivate the daily experiences you desire and deserve. Now that you are clear on which season you would like to lean into, it is time to get into the how. Here are some activities to help you achieve your desired goals within your current season of life.

Routine Wisdom: Surrendering to Your Season Creates a Realistic Routine

When your routine supports your current season of life, it is manageable and provides access to more ease and joy. Instead of playing tug-of-war between life as it is and how you want it to be, your routine steers you to what's needed most in this moment. The following activities will help you gauge how to lean in.

Acknowledge Your Feelings

Your feelings matter. Too often, we brush aside what we feel because we either fear the good feelings won't last or the uncomfortable feelings are too much to bear. The problem is, dismissing your feelings won't make them go away. When you suppress your emotions, usually the opposite happens, and your feelings intensify and grow. This may not sound so bad if your feelings are positive and joyful, but if they're more uncomfortable or draining, you can start to become resentful. Your feelings lead to your actions, and your actions will impact the success or failure of routine building. So acknowledging your feelings is the first step toward creating successful routines that lead to a fulfilled life.

Whether you are elated because you finally feel equipped to manage your life or you are deeply frustrated because you feel stuck in life, you have the right to feel any emotion that comes up for you. Feel the emotion, sit with it, then process it. Below are activities that will help you process the emotions you are feeling in this current season. You can use this activity whenever feelings arise that make you uncomfortable or uneasy.

Activity #1: It Is Understandable

Think about how you are feeling at this moment. What is one emotion that comes to mind? Now complete this sentence: It is understandable that I feel [insert emotion] because_____.

Example: It is understandable that I feel overwhelmed because I have so much to do and little help.

Activity #2: Mindfulness Exercise

Whenever an emotion arises, get curious about how you're feeling by asking yourself this question: How am I feeling at this moment and why? This exercise can help ground you, assign meaning to the emotion, and oftentimes, connect you with the beauty and wonder of your current season.

Stick to the Facts

Data is a strong tool that can help you get out of your head and into the reality of a situation. Our minds are beautiful, but they can also keep us stuck in a repetitive cycle of uneasy thoughts if we are not careful. Stating the facts of your current season of life can provide information you may have otherwise overlooked that could shed light on the truth of your season and possibly lead to a resolution.

Activity: Complete a 24-Hour Time Study

Over the course of a typical day, record every action you take from the time you wake up until the time you go to sleep. For every action, be sure to also record how you are feeling in the moment. Completing a time study in this way provides truthful evidence of what's working and helps to guide you toward where a routine may best support your life.

FYI: There are phone applications that can make completing a time study easier, including ATracker Time Tracker, Hours Time Tracking, and Life Cycle.

Practice Gratitude

Exercising gratitude on a consistent basis greatly impacted my ability to notice the good in challenging seasons and tough moments. This is a simple concept that awakens you to an extraordinary perspective. When you stop and state what you are grateful for, this allows you to move beyond the past, take a step back from the future, and stand in the present moment. Mindfulness is a key factor to accepting and acknowledging your current situation.

Practicing gratitude also gives you a positive perspective, which comes in handy when you are faced with difficult moments. Gratitude can be used as a tool to shift your focus from what's wrong to what's good, giving you the courage and outlook to keep going. When you find yourself having a rough moment, you can practice gratitude. Starting to feel frustrated or anxious? Acknowledge the feeling and state what you are grateful for in the moment. This was the hallmark that allowed me to lean into my life fully, and it can do the same for you.

Activities to Spark Gratitude

1. Below or on a sheet of paper, write a list of the things, people, and places you are grateful for in this current season of life.

....

....

....

....

....

....

2. Every morning when you open your eyes, say three things you are grateful for before starting your day.

3. While walking through your home or engaging in a specific routine, identify things or actions that spark joy or gratitude.

Whether you want to make minimal improvements or create a drastic change, hopefully now you have a deeper appreciation for the current season you're in. You are right where you need to be, and if you begin to question this, remember there are tools to help. Acknowledge your feelings, state the facts, and practice gratitude consistently. Keeping a positive perspective will help you create joy and assemble the best routine for your life at this very moment.

Chapter 5
COMPONENTS OF AN EFFECTIVE ROUTINE

Contrary to popular belief, creativity is not absent from routine. It's actually needed to create effective routines. According to the *Merriam-Webster Dictionary*, "create" means "to bring something into existence." With routine building you can do just that—activate your inner creativity and bring into existence the routines that will help you achieve your desired outcomes. The sky's the limit. What you do in your routine and how it flows depends entirely on your creativity. This is what makes routine building so much fun. You become the artist of your own life by choosing exactly what's needed for your routines; you are painting the picture of the life you desire.

Typically, routines are created in two ways: with preparation or on the fly. You may think one is better than the other, but I've come to understand that they both have advantages depending on the individual and the circumstance. More importantly, the most integral part of creating any routine, whether on a whim or not, is to do so from an intentional place. Yes, creativity is important but intentionality is the hallmark of a successful routine and without it, you may find yourself spinning your wheels and stuck in an unhealthy pattern on repeat.

It can be helpful to think of your routine as an outline rather than a script. An outline gives you direction but doesn't restrict your creativity. You'll find that a more flexible routine is a more manageable one.

Throughout the process, it's also important to start where you are and avoid overthinking. Keep your outcome as the focal point; it will help to determine the steps of your routine and directly impacts your ability to maintain it. There are simple ways to identify the right action steps to include in your routine. The process starts with you.

Your Routine, Your Rules

I remember the day I shared my laundry routine on social media. After numerous attempts and frustrating moments with laundry routines inspired by others, I decided to create my very own. After sharing what I like to call My 3-Day Laundry Routine, I received countless messages from women saying that they tried out my new routine, and it was mind-blowing. Rather than doing a load of laundry a day, I decided to spread out my routine between three days. It goes like this, wash laundry on Day 1, fold laundry on Day 3, put away laundry on Day 3. After receiving so much positive feedback on my laundry routine, I realized creating routines specific to my life produced a better outcome.

Here's my question to you: What do you want your routine to be, outside of how others structure their routines and beyond the routines you learned in the past? It's easy to get wrapped up in the status quo. Gaining inspiration from others can be extremely helpful, but it's always important to consider if the actions in their routine work for you as an individual. To stay in alignment with your wants and needs, here are a few questions to ask yourself when inspired by others.

- What do I truly think of this routine?

- Can I see myself consistently doing this routine?

- Can my current life handle this routine?

The routines you create can only serve you if they are created with you in mind. For some routines, such as cleaning and cooking, it will be simple to decide which actions are needed. Flexible routines like self-care and planning can be more challenging to put together, especially if you don't know which actions will best meet your needs. Whenever you become stuck at what steps to include, focus on the purpose of the routine and think of things you enjoy doing. This combination can help you determine the actions of your routine.

For example, imagine you are stuck creating a planning routine. If your desire is to feel prepared and you enjoy organizing your day by time, a step of your routine could be to time-block, or divide your day into blocks, noting when you'll complete specific tasks. Don't be afraid to think outside the box and do things that seem unorthodox. You may think there's only one or a few ways to do a routine, but allow your curiosity and creativity to call this into question. Make it your mission to blow your own mind when creating your routine.

Determining Your Win

When creating routines, align the actions with the result you're looking for. Your first step is to determine the outcome or win you want to achieve. You can think about this as reverse engineering. By starting with your win, deciding your course of action will be simpler and the process of routine building more enjoyable.

Your win can be a tangible result or an intangible feeling, it's totally up to you. You can ask yourself, "What would make this routine a win for me?" If you determine your win will have a tangible outcome, it's important to make it as specific as possible. Specificity makes choosing your actions more straightforward. If your win is a feeling you want to experience, choose actions that align with that specific feeling. Below are a few examples of routines and specific wins for each.

Routine > Win > Actions

⇨ **Kitchen Routine**

Purpose/Win: Clean dishes, countertops, and floor

Suggested steps: Wash dishes > Wipe countertops > Sweep floor

⇨ **Tidy Routine**

Purpose/Win: Everything off the floor and back in its designated place

Suggested steps: Clear floor of items > Put items back in respective place

⇨ Morning Routine

Purpose/Win: To feel energized and productive

Suggested steps: Movement > Shower > Plan day

⇨ Bedtime Routine

Purpose/Win: To feel calm and peaceful

Suggested steps: Journal > Meditation

Here are some blank templates to fill out your own routines with specific wins:

⇨ .... **Routine**

Purpose/Win:..

....

Steps:..

....

....

....

....

⇨ .... **Routine**

Purpose/Win:..

....

Steps:..

....

....

....

....

⇨ .... **Routine**

Purpose/Win:...

....

Steps:..

....

....

....

....

⇨ .... **Routine**

Purpose/Win:...

....

Steps:..

....

....

....

....

During the creation phase, it's extremely important to focus on your actions. Your actions drive your outcome, and without true intentionality, you can find yourself knee-deep in a routine that yields a poor result. Routines aren't about popularity or perfection. They are here to steer you on course toward living a life you are passionate about and proud of.

Four Considerations

Remember to create an outline rather than a script, match your actions to your desired outcome, and then take into account four unique and powerful considerations: make it simple, make it realistic, make it flexible, and make it fun.

Make It Simple

The first consideration is to make your routine simple. The simpler your routine, the easier it will be to manage and the more likely you will be to sustain it.

When I created my first morning routine, I remember reading articles and books that said my routine needed to include between five and eight steps if I wanted to start my day off right. I recall thinking to myself, "How in the world am I going to keep this up?" I tried one of the suggested routines and not even a week into it, I gave up completely. It was extremely complicated to keep up with all the actions every morning, and I couldn't manage it. I don't want this to be you. Keep your routine simple and watch how much easier it becomes.

One way to make your routine simple is to add actions that are uncomplicated and lessen the amount of actions in your routine. Think about it this way: Do the actions in your routine require a lot of effort, or are they pretty easy for you to maintain? If you tend to struggle with simplicity, here's a rule of thumb: If you can easily memorize and repeat the steps of your routine, it's simple enough.

As an example, let's compare Brittney's and Kim's morning routines. Brittney's morning routine includes the following actions: take a shower, brush teeth, pick out clothes for the day, make coffee, journal, and go for a walk outside. Kim's morning routine includes the following actions: journal, plan day, and exercise. Do you see the difference in their routines? Kim's routine is much simpler than Brittney's, which means Kim is more likely to keep her routine going. To simplify Brittney's routine, she could take out shower, brush teeth, and pick out clothes, since these are habitual actions she is more than likely to do every morning. This would lessen the number of steps in her routine and make it more manageable and more likely for her to maintain it.

Remember, keep your routine simple. I know creating something new can spark joy and enthusiasm, but try not to become overzealous in the process. A simple routine equals a simple life, and a simple life brings about more peace of mind. Now that you've learned a few tips for simplifying your routine, it's time to move on to the next important consideration, which is making it realistic.

Make It Realistic

Ever create a routine that you struggled to keep going just a few days into starting it? It could be that your routine wasn't realistic enough. Making your routine realistic means fitting it into your current lifestyle and season. Way too often, we struggle to remain in the present moment. We are usually dwelling in the past or too focused on the future. This doesn't help to create realistic routines. Your routine must serve your life right now, so you instantly reap the rewards. This makes you more likely to maintain it.

To help you avoid making the mistake of creating an unrealistic routine, here's a story that shares how being overzealous led to an unmanageable routine:

Tiffany is a mom of a newborn. At three months postpartum, she decides to create an exercise routine that includes strength training and intense cardio workouts, although she hasn't exercised in over a year. She begins her new exercise routine and after only two days, she realizes she needs to start slow and begins creating a more realistic exercise routine.

This story is common. Sometimes we are so eager to make changes that we inadvertently sabotage our success. There's nothing wrong with wanting to make progress, but progress starts with accepting our present situation. Whether you are facing multiple challenges or you're completely content, you must accept your life for what it is. If you fail to do so, you will struggle to create a routine that meets your current needs. To get you started in the right direction, below is a suggested activity to help you create realistic routines.

Create a Later List

On My Later List on page 75 or a blank sheet of paper, write out actions that you want to include in your routine. Don't hold back. Once you have a list of actions, go through each action one by one and decide if it would be best to add now or later when your life can better handle it. Circle the actions that can be done later. This is your later list. Here is an example of a Later List for a morning routine:

Initial List
- Journal
- Plan
- Exercise
- Read
- Meditate

Later List

- Journal—can add this to bedtime routine

- Read—will hold off until I have more time to spare

- Meditate—will start once I find a meditation app I like

Final List

- Plan

- Exercise

After you think about ways to make your routine realistic, the next stop is to uncover ways to make it flexible.

My Later List

Make It Flexible

When I first started creating intentional routines, I thought they needed to be super structured or things would fall apart. With experience, I have come to learn that this is far from the truth. I've realized the stricter my routines were, the less I enjoyed them because I felt like I was putting too much pressure on myself. After many failed attempts with rigid routines, I began creating flexible routines that led to more freedom and ease in my life.

A flexible routine means having the ability to change your course of action if you choose to do so. If you consider yourself a spontaneous person who loves to go with the flow, having a flexible routine is important. Even if you're naturally routine oriented, a flexible routine can also benefit you. As humans we are creatures of habit, but we also love choice. Flexible routines give you the power to choose and can lessen the possibility of routine fatigue and boredom, two things that can hinder you from maintaining your routine.

There are two ways to add flexibility to your routine: you can make the timing of your routine flexible or the actions in your routine flexible. Before we dive into each, it's important to understand not all routines will allow for flexibility. For example, a laundry routine is likely to be more restrictive than a self-care routine.

Let's start with timing. Think about whether your routine can be done at different times of the day. For example, if you usually do your laundry routine first thing in the morning, flexibility offers the possibility for it to be done midday or at night as well. Or maybe, if you usually do your weekly planning routine on Sunday, there could be room for your planning to fit into your schedule on another day of the week. Identifying different times your routine can be done is very helpful if you have an unpredictable schedule or for days that don't go as planned.

Another way to create freeing routines is to focus on the flexibility of your actions. This means you have freedom of choice within your routines. Let's be honest, our moods can change from day to day, and it's great if you can create a routine to accommodate these changes. You may wake up and want to do a different exercise than what's included in your routine. If you have a routine that allows for choice, you won't feel like a failure when you naturally change your mind and desire to do something slightly different. Broader actions create flexible routines. To give you an idea of how to make your routines flexible, check out the list below.

Restrictive Action	Flexible Action
Yoga	Exercise
Walk	Move my body
Coffee	Beverage
Sweep	Clear floor
Read book	Read
Load dishwasher	Clean dishes
Cook dinner	Feed family

Like I said before, flexibility may not be possible for every routine, but it can be helpful to consider, especially if you crave freedom of choice or have a fluctuating schedule.

Now that you've learned the benefit of flexible routines, it's time to move on to the last consideration in the creation phase, making your routine fun.

Make It Fun

Making your routine fun is the last consideration when creating your routine, but it's definitely not the least. Fun is a must when it comes to creating any and every routine. It is the spark that will get you going and keep you going on days when you want to call it quits. You will be doing your routine often, and to keep it that way, having an enjoyable routine that lightens your mood is extremely important.

People always ask me how I stick to routines. The answer is simple: I make them fun. Because routines are often referenced as mundane and boring, many people make the mistake of excluding enjoyment during routine building. I made this exact mistake early on and quickly noticed that if my routines lacked joy, they didn't last. This insight has changed the way I create routines today and has had a huge impact on my life.

There are two ways to think about making your routine fun: focus the fun inside the routine or outside the routine. Focusing the fun inside means including actions within your routine that are enjoyable for you. For example, if you are creating a bedtime routine, try including actions that will get you excited to do your routine. This could be lighting your favorite scented candle, turning on soothing music, or snuggling up in a warm blanket. It's best if the actions you choose are specific to you and raise your happiness meter. This simple adjustment can make the transition easier when starting a new routine.

Another way to focus the fun inside the routine is to enjoy the result of your routine. This means the win can be your fun. The instant gratification that comes from a high-energy Zumba class, reading a few pages of a captivating book, or taking a walk in a different neighborhood can act as a catalyst and motivate you to start and maintain your routine. Focusing on the result can even serve as a fun distraction at times. However if you are creating a routine where the actions can't be changed to be more enjoyable or the result doesn't drive you, focusing the fun outside your routine can help.

Focusing the fun outside means pairing your routine with enjoyable activities. If you enjoy listening to music, you could turn on your favorite playlist while you clean the bathroom. If you're a coffee lover like me, making yourself a nice cup of coffee when doing your weekly planning routine is a great way to add in pleasure. While you fold clothes, you could catch up on your favorite show or talk to your bestie on the phone. Indulging in fun activities while you do your routine makes maintaining it less of a challenge. There are plenty of activities you can pair with your routine to make it entertaining. Below is a list of inspirational ideas.

Fun Activities:
- Light a candle.
- Talk to your friend on the phone.
- Raise shades to let in light.
- Have your family help.
- Use items you enjoy, such as your favorite cleaning products, a cute planner, or a new kitchen gadget.
- Listen to a podcast.
- Watch a movie or TV show.
- Listen to music.
- Make it a game or challenge.

Take these components into consideration when creating any routine. Simplicity keeps you focused, realistic routines keep you grounded, flexible routines create choice, and fun is key to a lasting routine. You are the rule maker for your routines, so keep your wants and needs in the forefront at all times. The creation phase of routine building can be simple and enjoyable. Get creative and think outside of the box; your creativity can lead to the most incredible routines.

Putting It All Together

Whether you want to overhaul your routine completely or make slight changes to an existing one, you now know what you need to create amazing routines that are simple, realistic, flexible, and fun. For more direction to guide you in creating your routine, check out the step-by-step process below. All you need are the templates provided on the next page (or a blank sheet of paper) and a pen to get started.

Routines from Scratch example:

Step 1. Recognize Your Win (Determine your outcome.)

Step 2. Select Your Steps (Choose action steps that lead to the desired outcome.)

Step 3. Consider Your Components (Take into account four components: simple, realistic, flexible, fun.)

Step 4. Alter Your Actions (Change actions as needed.)

Revamping Your Routine example:

Step 1. Recognize Your Win (Determine your outcome.)

Step 2. Study Your Steps (Review current action steps to ensure they lead to the desired outcome.)

Step 3. Consider Your Components (Take into account four components: simple, realistic, flexible, fun.)

Step 4. Alter Your Actions (Change actions as needed.)

New Routine

1. Outcome: ....

....

2. Steps: ....

....

3. Components: ....

....

....

....

....

4. Alter your actions: ....

....

....

Revised Routine

1. Outcome: ....

....

2. Review current steps: ....

....

3. Consider your components: ....

....

....

....

....

4. Alter your actions: ....

....

....

Problem: Timmeshia was feeling the weight of being a work-from-home mom of three small children. She knew she needed more structure for herself and children but didn't know where to start when it came to building routines.

What helped: I taught Timmeshia what components to consider when building routines (simplicity, realistic expectations, flexibility, and fun). I specifically mentioned how routines are wellness activities for a healthy life. I invited her to step away from how she was taught to do things and instead focus on what would make managing her life easier for her, even if they seemed unorthodox and different from what she was accustomed to.

Outcome: The invitation to reframe her view of routines and break away from how she was taught to do certain routines helped her see a new and better normal for her life. She began creating routines specific to her unique lifestyle such as a morning kitchen routine and weekly home-planning routine. She now thrives on daily and weekly routines that keep her in flow.

"Ashley's teachings on routine building single-handedly transformed my understanding and perspective of routines. Learning that routines can be a form of wellness awakened a desire within me to get creative and build my very own. The depth of truth within the pages of this handbook encouraged me throughout my unique routine-building process. So much so, I know that I will be referring to these pages again and

again as seasons of life change and the need arises to revamp or create new routines. One concept in particular that has given me a sense of peace in my life and home was learning that routines can be fun, flexible, realistic, and simple. This small token of wisdom has radically changed how I show up in my home and in my life! I'm truly grateful for Ashley's wisdom."

Chapter 6
ROUTINE CREATION FAQS

Creating any routine takes intentional effort and time, and if you're not careful, you can get sidetracked and unintentionally fall back into old unhealthy routines. Now that you're in the creation phase, there may be questions that arise as you sort through what's most important to include in your routine. Browse the most frequently asked questions that arise when creating an ideal routine.

Q: Where do I start when creating a routine?

A: After you decide which routine you will be creating, the first step is to determine your desired outcome. Your outcome can be a tangible result or an intangible feeling that you want to experience. By knowing the outcome you desire, you will be better able to select actions for your routine that align with the result you want to achieve.

When determining your outcome, it is best to be as specific as possible. Specificity will help you choose the steps of your routine with ease. For example, let's say you decide to create a kitchen routine. A nonspecific outcome could be "a clean kitchen," whereas a specific outcome could be "clean dishes and clear countertops." Don't overthink this. Just remember that it's best if you know the outcome of your routine before deciding what to include within it.

Once you're clear on the outcome, you can begin to select steps to include in the routine that lead to your intended result. Below is an example of a kitchen routine with the outcome of clean dishes and clear countertops.

⇨ **Kitchen Routine**

Suggested steps: Unload dishwasher > Load dishwasher > Wipe kitchen surfaces

Frequency: Daily

Timing: 30 minutes

Purpose: Clean dishes and countertops

Q: What are important factors to consider when creating a routine?

A: When creating any routine, the four major considerations are keeping it simple, realistic, flexible, and fun. Each consideration brings a different element to your routine so you are more equipped to maintain and enjoy it. Below is a brief overview of each. For a deeper review of each consideration, see Chapter 5.

Simple: Simplify or decrease the actions in your routine.

Realistic: Be sure your routine represents you and serves your specific lifestyle.

Flexible: Broad actions create more flexibility (think of your actions as an outline versus a script).

Fun: Spice up your routine by incorporating actions you enjoy or pairing your routine with activities that spark joy.

Q: Should I include a specific number of steps or actions within my routine?

A: The amount of actions in your routine is totally up to you. Keep in mind that the most successful routines are those that you can easily manage. If having many steps feels doable, go for it. To lessen the potential of creating a complicated routine, choose intentional actions that are completely necessary. Do away with the fluff and stick to specific steps that will give you the outcome you're looking for.

If you struggle with simplicity or find it difficult to limit the actions in your routine, ask yourself a few simple questions.

1. Is each step within my routine truly necessary?

2. Could any of the steps be combined to form one step?

3. Do I believe I can easily manage repeating the steps in my routine?

4. Does the routine include any habitual actions that can be removed?

Q: I need a routine ASAP, Is there a quick way to create one?

A: Refer to Chapter 5 for specific steps when creating a new or revamped routine. Ultimately, to create a routine in a hurry, it will come down to three factors:

1. Being clear on the desired outcome

2. Selecting steps

3. Not overthinking the process

Even if you want to create a routine in a hurry, understand that the best routines take time. A rushed routine leads to rushed results, which will not be helpful if you need less stress and more order in your life. It can be hard to remain patient, but the reward of purposeful decision-making is well worth it.

Q: Should I write my routine down on paper?

A: Yes, it can be helpful to write your routine down as you're creating it. Your mind can only hold on to so much information. Plus, writing your routine on paper is a great way to examine its elements. On paper, you can easily play around with the order of the steps, erase steps, or add in new steps until you get to a routine that works for you. You'll have it as a reference for the future.

Q: Help, what should I include in my routine?

A: If you're stuck deciding which actions to place in your routine, start with determining the desired outcome or win. Then consider what you would enjoy doing in your routine. How can you get to your result in a way that feels good to you and aligns with your natural flow? Here's a formula that can help.

Desire + Like = Action (Desired Outcome + Things You Enjoy = Potential Action Step)

Examples:

1. Calm start to my day (desire) + writing (like) = Journal (action)

2. More energy (desire) + moving my body (like) = Walk (action)

3. Better sleep (desire) + listening to music (like) = Sound therapy (action)

You try it:

Desire:..**+**

Like:..**=**

Desired Outcome:...

Desire:..**+**

Like:..**=**

Desired Outcome:...

Desire:..**+**

Like:..**=**

Desired Outcome:...

Resist the urge to overthink this part. Yes, it's important to create an intentional routine, but perfection isn't a requirement. Add a few actions you believe will get you the outcome you're looking for and move on. You can always change the actions in your routine whenever you feel the need.

Q: I'm in need of inspiration. Can you share examples of routines you've created?

A: These are some routines I've personally had in my life and routines I've witnessed other women create. You'll see a range of possibilities in routines, which will help you gain inspiration. But try not to mimic. It's best when your routine is created specifically for your needs and with you in mind. When reading over the routines below, ask yourself if the action suits you and your lifestyle at this moment. Get creative and do what works for you.

⇨ My 3-Day Laundry Routine

Suggested steps:

Day 1: Wash and Dry Laundry (usually three full-size loads excluding bedding)

Day 2: Fold Laundry (Clothes can get wrinkled from sitting in basket for a full day, which I'm comfortable with. Folded clothing stays in baskets and is placed in bedrooms to be put away the next day.)

Day 3: Put Away Laundry (folded clothes are put into their respective places)

Frequency: Weekly

Timing: 3 consecutive days (time will vary depending on the amount of laundry)

Purpose: Simplify laundry and make the process more manageable.

⇨ Morning Routine

Suggested steps: Gratitude practice > Prayer > Journal

Frequency: Daily in morning

Timing: 10 to 20 minutes

Purpose: Mindfulness activities to strengthen mental health, because a strong and optimistic mindset usually leads to a successful day. Starting the morning being present has a positive ripple effect throughout the day.

⇨ Planning Routine

Suggested steps: Brain dump > Decide on top three priorities > Schedule tasks

Frequency: Weekly

Timing: ~ 20 minutes

Purpose: Great way to stay proactive and intentional with your time and energy. The brain dump clears the mind to improve decision-making. Deciding the top three priorities gives specific areas of focus for the week. The remaining tasks may be scheduled in a manner in which they can be accomplished alongside the priorities.

⇨ Evening Routine

Suggested steps: Listen to music > Exercise (at-home workout) > Get ready for bed

Frequency: Before every work day (usually four days per week)

Timing: ~ 2 hours

Purpose: Improve sleep

Q: I'm creating a routine for someone else. Is it best they be involved?

A: Absolutely. When creating routines for others, it is very helpful to have them assist in the process if they can. Getting the person involved increases the likelihood that they will enjoy and maintain the new routine. Whether this routine is for a small child or an elderly family member, if they are mentally and emotionally mature to communicate their desires, give them the opportunity. Getting the person involved gives them more stake in the process as well as the outcome. Work together as a team to create a routine they'll love. For example, if you're helping a teenager create an after-school routine, it helps to communicate about after-school activities and clubs they're involved in so you can work around those times and choose appropriate actions they will be able to manage. Similarly, if you are helping your elderly family member start a gardening routine, you can collaborate by going with them to the nursery to choose their favorite flowers to plant and deciding which days of the week would be best to care for the garden.

Q: What's the difference between creating a routine from scratch and revamping a routine?

A: The main difference is in the sequence of the routine. Creating a routine from scratch is similar to working with a blank sketchbook. You can decide what you want to draw on the page. It provides more room for creativity and lessens limitations. It's likely you will spend more time creating your routine, but ultimately you, are starting from a completely blank slate, unlike revamping a routine.

When revamping a routine, you already have a blueprint, but it needs alterations. In this case, the current actions will guide and help you understand the new direction of your routine. You can spend less time revamping a routine because you can apply important considerations to the current routine and alter as desired. Here's an example of my revamped evening routine.

⇨ Past Evening Routine

Steps: Family time, dinner, put kids to bed, shower

Frequency: 5 days a week

Timing: 2 hours

Purpose: To transition easily from evening to bedtime

⇨ Revamped Evening Routine

Steps: Dinner, family time, shower

Frequency: 4 days a week (on my work days)

Timing: 1.5 hours

Purpose: To help me have more time to prepare the night before a workday

I needed to alter my evening routine due to transitioning back to work full time. I removed one step by asking my husband to put the kids to bed and switched the order of steps so it was more realistic with my work schedule.

Overall, neither is more supreme than the other; it all depends on which route you want to take.

You try it now:

⇨ Past .... Routine

Steps: ....

....

Frequency: ....

Timing: ....

Purpose: ....

....

....

....

⇨ **Revamped** .... **Routine**
Steps: ....

....

Frequency: ....

Timing: ....

Purpose: ....

....

....

....

Q: Once I create a routine, how do I know it will work?

A: Unfortunately, after creating a routine, you will never know for certain if it will work until you put it into action. I remember my first attempt at an intentional morning routine failed because I assumed I had more time than I actually had. Once I started the routine, I realized I didn't have enough time for thoughtful journaling and planning my day. I quickly revamped this routine, which made my mornings smoother and less anxiety provoking. I've also had the opposite happen. After returning to work after having my first child, I started an exercise routine that included exercising in the evening. I did not think this would work because I figured I would be too tired to exercise after work and caring for a new baby. I was surprised when this routine lasted longer than I expected; plus, it actually helped me sleep better.

Trial and error is okay when creating your routine. It's a normal part of routine building that is hard to escape. Be intentional and trust you know what you need for your life. You will create an amazing routine, and if you don't, give yourself permission to go back to the drawing board.

Part 3
PROTECT YOUR PEACE
(Maintaining Routines)

Chapter 7
RECOGNIZE YOUR RESISTANCE

Let's be real, maintaining a routine isn't the easiest thing in the world. I've learned a major key to success is in managing your expectations. Once a routine starts, we tend to expect a lot from ourselves, and when we don't meet those expectations, this often leads to feelings of failure and a lack of self-trust. Holding onto these unwanted and untruthful feelings will not help us when it comes to maintaining our routines. Instead of having the expectation that your routine will go perfectly, it can be helpful to expect that you will simply try again if it doesn't.

If you're anything like me, you've started and abandoned many routines in your life. This experience can lead some people to think it is impossible to maintain routines. However, in my opinion, this isn't the truth. Keeping a routine going may not be easy, but the strategies and principles taught in this handbook will make the process much simpler.

In workshops I host, I teach women how to create and maintain routines. During these workshops, I always ask the women to explain what prompted them to attend. I remember one workshop in particular, when an attendee answered with, "I'm not routine-oriented, but I know I need a routine for my family so we can have more order around here." This is an answer I've heard more times than I can count. Each time I hear this, I can almost guarantee why this woman has struggled to maintain routines in her life: Her perspective is not in alignment with her desired outcome. The belief that she is "not a routine person" creates resistance and malalignment, although she wants to use routines to help.

For routines to work, you must believe you are capable of maintaining them. Remove the roadblock that says routines are only for type A people who love buying the latest planner. This is a total myth, and holding onto this belief is hurting your potential success. If you relate to this point of view and you doubt that routines can work because you've had many failed attempts, I invite you to look at your missteps through a different lens.

In my experience, what you see as failure is actually a sign of malalignment with your natural rhythm. Introducing a routine into your life should run parallel with who you are. Routines can be maintained by anyone and everyone, including yourself. Take pride in this and begin to believe routines can positively impact your life in a way that works for you and with you.

Here's an affirmation to help: "I am naturally flowing in routine."

Now I invite you to do a personal reflection. If you struggle with the belief that you are inconsistent, it can be helpful to take note of the ways you are already consistent with your routines. Think about what patterns you have been able to maintain daily and weekly. I'll bet you're more consistent than you think.

Daily Patterns

....

....

....

....

....

....

....

Weekly Patterns

....

....

....

....

....

....

....

....

Progress Is Progress

If you haven't heard this before, I want to be the first to inform you that you are not required to do your entire routine every single day. There, I said it. I'm what many would call a recovering perfectionist and retired overachiever. I know a little too much about the all-or-nothing mindset that cripples joy and progress. Routines aren't black and white; they are a rainbow of possibilities.

There will be days when you can't do your routine in its entirety or you'll need to prioritize certain routines over others. This isn't a golden ticket to do nothing; instead, it is a reminder that doing part of your routine is better than skipping it for the day. For example, your future self will thank you for washing the clothes, although you weren't able to fold and put them away. It's all progress, and there's always another opportunity to complete the entire routine. Moving beyond the all-or-nothing mindset takes practice. Remember, progress is progress no matter how small.

Remember this phrase as you're practicing: "Praise your progress until you can celebrate completion."

Why So Serious?

Another roadblock that can creep into maintaining any routine is the tendency to take routines too seriously. This can lead to routine fatigue and avoidance. You've learned that fun is a major consideration that can motivate you to stay consistent. Continue to keep this in mind and if your routine is getting a bit stale, think of ways to spice it up, such as sipping a glass of wine as you cook or using fun stickers to decorate your planner. Adopting routines doesn't have to turn you into a boring robot. Routines are meant to help you live with ease, not suck the fun out of life.

Being an adult doesn't mean you can't enjoy and take pleasure in your life. I understand adulting can be hard, but let's not make it harder by turning routines into rules and overwhelming ourselves with the small details. I'm a stickler for wanting things to be done right, but I've realized there's no one right way to do a routine, and removing this restriction has helped me loosen up and invite joy into my everyday tasks. When all else fails, turn up the fun. You'll notice a huge difference in your ability to maintain your routine; plus, you'll actually want to keep it going.

Compassion and Acknowledgment

If you're ready for a routine that lasts beyond one week, much of your success will depend on how you treat yourself throughout the process. Maintaining routines comes with its challenges and is not a perfect journey. Pressuring yourself to get it just right or deeming yourself inconsistent when you miss a day or two of your routine is the quickest way to call it quits. Being kind and compassionate with yourself when your routine doesn't go according to plan grants you permission to try again and is imperative to keep it going.

Constant acknowledgment of your routine is also meaningful to your success. It isn't enough to do your routine and move on with your day as usual. To acknowledge your routine means to validate the value it's adding to your life. Outwardly expressing and acknowledging the impact of your routine is like sending a message to your brain to keep going because it begins to recognize the routine as a major factor in your life. Instead of doing your routine and proceeding with your day, pause and state what your routine means to you and how it has positively impacted your life. Below is an example of what acknowledging your routine could look like.

Example:

- You just finished doing your morning routine.
- Stop what you're doing.
- Acknowledge your routine by saying "This routine made me feel [fill in the blank]." "I'm so happy I did this routine because it helped me [fill in the blank]."

Compassion with yourself and acknowledgment of your routine are often overlooked, but they are powerful in helping your routine last. Remember, you are allowed to miss a day of your routine because there will always be another day and opportunity. And once you do start back, constantly acknowledge the value your routine has on your life. Keep this in mind as you start new routines and you'll begin to see the difference it makes.

Routine Wisdom: Be Kind to Yourself

I used to be my worst critic, beating myself up when I missed a day of my routine and wondering why I could never stick to it. After diving into some personal development resources, I learned a valuable lesson I didn't know I needed. I realized that my negative behavior toward myself when things didn't work out as planned was dramatically impacting my progress. I decided at that moment to begin to treat myself with more compassion when I would skip my routine for a day or two. Instead of focusing on what I didn't do, I validated the feelings around skipping my routine, acknowledged the reason for doing so, and made the choice to try again the next day. This small but powerful adjustment changed the trajectory of my future routines. I'm more equipped to maintain my routines, and I've developed a better relationship with myself.

Common Routine Roadblocks

When it comes to maintaining your routine, from time to time, roadblocks will get in the way. This is normal. While some roadblocks are unavoidable, not all of them are a problem, but rather more of a red flag, a sign that there's a deeper issue that needs to be addressed. By recognizing what stands in the way of a successful routine, you can improve the likelihood of maintaining it. Below are some common roadblocks and how to proceed if you encounter them.

Time Conflicts

How many times have you missed your routine because it conflicted with another important commitment? This can be frustrating and cause you to get off track with your routine. Luckily, there are a few ways to prevent schedule conflicts from interfering with your routine. One way is to make your routine flexible, especially when it comes to the time of day your routine will be done. A flexible routine that allows you to shift your actions to a different time can eliminate the need to skip it for that day. For example, if your routine is to ride your exercise bike at 9:00 a.m., but you realize you have a doctor's appointment at that time, you can consider riding your exercise bike in the evening instead.

Another way to adjust to a schedule conflict is to be proactive. If you know ahead of time you will not be available to do your routine because it conflicts with another commitment, you can either plan for someone else to do the routine for you or do the routine ahead of schedule. Whether you miss a day or not, being proactive gives you control over how you utilize your time, and this can motivate you to continue on with your routine.

Don't let time conflicts throw you off your game. Changes in schedule are a part of life so instead of working hard to avoid them, try to move with the changes and adjust your routines accordingly. Remaining flexible will strengthen your consistency and keep your routine thriving.

Low Energy

Experiencing a tiring day is often a huge roadblock for maintaining routines. It is understandable when you don't have the energy to invest in your routine, but it can also feel uneasy to skip doing something that greatly impacts your mood, home, or family. Low energy does not automatically disqualify you from maintaining your routine. Energy is all around and by knowing ways to tap into yours, consistency with your routine is possible.

Before sharing how you can maximize your energy, recognize that low energy is very different from exhaustion. When you are mentally, physically, or emotionally exhausted from a long day at work, a full day with your kids, or dealing with an illness, rest is required. You can only give from the energy you have, so if your tank is empty, the best routine for you to do is rest. Once you have restored your energy, you can then get on with life and your routines as usual.

What can you do if tiredness is getting in your way? First, pinpoint what type of tiredness you're feeling. Are you physically, mentally, or emotionally tired? Once you can indicate where your low energy stems from, you can decide on the best course of action. Below is a list of each state of tiredness and suggestions within each for restoring your energy to remain consistent with your routine. You will also notice how each suggestion adds value to your life.

Physically Tired

- Exercise.
- Dance to music.
- Give yourself a massage.
- Stretch.
- Get up and start moving.

Mentally Tired

- Rest for a few minutes.
- Meditate.
- Sit in silence with the lights off.
- Decrease stimulation.
- Take a walk outside.
- Do a deep-breathing exercise.

Emotionally Tired

- Validate how you're feeling.
- Talk to someone you love and trust.
- Pray.
- Journal.
- Listen to uplifting music.

Routine Fatigue

Routine fatigue occurs when you no longer have any desire to do your routine. This can happen due to a prolonged period of maintaining a specific routine or boredom from a lack of fun in your routine. To overcome this, a change in your routine is necessary. Think of ideas for adding variety or including excitement and fun into your routine. You could make a playlist of your favorite dance songs to play during your workout or create a fun reward chart with your child for every day a routine is completed. If your routine still works for your life, remain cautious about overhauling your entire routine. A slight change can refresh your routine while still including the components that have helped you to thrive. For example, clean your bedroom with the windows up or fold clothes while talking to your best friend. If this is a roadblock you find yourself at, in what ways can you make your routine different or exciting?

Sabotaging Behaviors

Self-sabotage is a major roadblock to consistency that frequently goes unnoticed. It's easy to become accustomed to unproductive habits that get in the way of your progress. Sabotage isn't an intentional choice but a natural response that can indicate a problem. Usually when you are avoiding your routine to do something that feels easier in the moment, this is a huge signal that something about your routine is off. For some perspective, sabotage can look like choosing to scroll social media for countless hours instead of doing your laundry routine or bingeing Netflix instead of getting your bedtime routine going. There's always a reason behind the avoidance and investigating the issue can lead you to engage in less sabotaging behaviors.

Consuming yourself with social media or TV isn't the only way sabotage shows up. Sabotage can be a sneaky culprit, especially if the activities you put in place of your routine are productive uses of your time. For example, organizing your pantry or working on your brand new business idea can seem harmless. Those actions alone are not a problem, but when you are using them to avoid doing your routine, they can stall your progress. Become aware of your sabotaging behaviors. What are your usual go-tos when you want to avoid doing important tasks? In what ways are you productive that you could easily fall prey to? These are great questions to ask yourself to get started on the right foot. Once you understand how you get in the way of your success, your success becomes more possible.

My Sabotaging Behaviors

....

....

....

....

....

....

....

Maintaining your routine won't come without its challenges. However, you can equip yourself with a strong mindset to help you stay the course. Avoid all-or-nothing thinking. Have fun with your routines, remain compassionate, and constantly acknowledge the value your routine adds. Lastly, keep in mind that roadblocks are part of the routine-building journey. Recognize the resistance and practice moving beyond it. Trust me, you're well on your way.

Chapter 8
TOOLS FOR STAYING ON TRACK

When you are starting a new routine or revamping an old one, there will be an adjustment period. Routine building is not an overnight process. It will take time for you to get accustomed to your new routine. In this chapter, I will discuss some helpful tools that will assist you with keeping the momentum going.

Here's some encouragement if you've experienced challenges with maintaining routines in the past. Please know it is not due to your inability. Rather, you may have been unaware of tools to help you along the way.

Here's a quick story for you. In the beginning of my routine-building journey, sticking to my routines was harder than I imagined. I was constantly falling off track, and I didn't understand why. So, I became the girl to do all the things. I tried everything I could think of to keep my routines going. Although it took time to troubleshoot the problem, I eventually realized I wasn't utilizing simple strategies available to me. Once I discovered these strategies, it was much easier for me to stay the course. Even now, I still use many of them to help keep me on track.

Both I and past customers have used these tried-and-true strategies as a way to maintain other things outside of routines. It is likely these strategies are not new to you but, possibly, they have been underutilized. For those that aren't your cup of tea, I suggest that you find another that works best to keep your routine thriving. As you go through each, take note of which ones you want to try out.

Reminders

Staying on track with your routine will require more than writing it down or declaring your new routine is here to stay. You will need to be reminded to do your routine and reminded often. Think about it. You make a million decisions each day, so the likelihood you'll remember to do a brand-new routine is slim. Plus, after the excitement of starting something new wears off, you'll need a way to keep your routine at the top of your mind. Here are three specific reminders that can be extremely useful in helping you to maintain your routine:

Visual Reminders

Once you start a routine, I know you have every intention to keep it going; however, forgetting to do your routine is possible, and it happens. This is where visual reminders can play a huge role. As they say, out of sight out of mind.

A rule of thumb is to be sure to place the visual reminder in an area or space you visit often. For example, when starting a morning routine, a great place to post a reminder could be your bathroom mirror. If you use a planner consistently, you may want to write a note inside to remind you to do your routine.

Some other visual reminders to help you stay on track include writing your routine down and posting it on the fridge, setting a phone notification to pop up, making a picture of your detailed routine your phone or computer background, or placing the items used in your routine within your eyesight. The more visual reminders you have, the more likely you will continue with the routine you've started.

Auditory Reminders

Auditory reminders can be just as powerful as visual reminders when used intentionally. Your phone can be a great auditory reminder. Set an alarm to go off at a certain time. This will prompt you to do your routine. You can also turn on calendar notification bells that ping when it's time to get started with your routine.

A useful trick that helps to capture my attention when setting alarms is to choose my favorite upbeat song as the alarm music instead of sticking with the presets on my phone. If this sounds helpful to you, it can give your alarm a personal feel and become a more enticing way to get you up and moving with your routine.

Social Reminders

Similar to accountability, social reminders use interaction with other people to help you keep momentum. Two types of social reminders are particularly helpful: perceived accountability and actual accountability. Perceived accountability usually happens when you declare to someone else that you will do a certain thing. This looks like telling your best friend you are committed to doing your exercise routine or sharing with your coworker about restarting your bedtime routine. This is perceived accountability because you haven't asked your friend and coworker to hold you accountable, but declaring your course of action makes you feel the need to follow through with what you said.

The second social reminder is actual accountability. This looks like joining an actual accountability group or asking someone to check up on your progress from time to time. Requesting accountability is a strong way to maintain your routine because as humans, we typically hate to admit our shortcomings. It can feel disappointing to go back on your word. Be cautious with how you use accountability because although it is a powerful tool for maintaining your routine, it can also become damaging if you lack compassion with yourself throughout the process.

When seeking accountability, use your family and friends for support or join groups or programs with others who have a similar goal as you. With the right accountability, you'll see a major difference in your consistency with the routine you start.

Reminders are a simple but extremely effective tool. When starting your routine, it's better to use as many reminders as you can. Think about which ones would be the best approach for you personally. If you are a visual learner, visual reminders would be a great place to start. Maybe you're someone who finds motivation by working alongside others. If so, social reminders could be impactful for you. Keep your routine in the forefront and you'll find much success along the way.

Rewards

Accomplishment is always sweeter when there's a reward in the end. Routines are no different. Knowing there's a reward on the other end of your routine can be a motivating factor for continued progress. The reward is totally up to you, but it must be something that incentivizes you to keep going. Rewards will look different from one routine to another and can change frequently depending on your mood. Review the three rewards below. Each one has its purpose and can prove helpful for staying consistent with your routine.

Treat Yourself

Who says routines can't come with goodies? Just as you may give a child a treat after a huge accomplishment, you can do the same for yourself to reward your hard work. I can remember indulging in a bottle of wine after a month of consistently sticking to my exercise routine. Maybe that wasn't the best choice after working my butt off to lose the weight, but it did challenge me to stay committed. Try gifting yourself something special after committing consistently to your routine. This could be buying yourself those shoes you've been eyeing online, pampering yourself with a spa day, or taking time to sit outside alone and bask in the warm sun. No treat is too big or too small, just make sure it's a reward that will inspire you to keep going. What will it be for you?

Praise Break

Rewarding yourself isn't just about gifts. You can also celebrate your consistency by praising your efforts. I learned this lesson early in motherhood. You cannot expect others to praise your progress, even if what you're doing is for their benefit. You must thank yourself and get comfortable with singing your own praises, saying phrases such as, "I rocked that" or "I'm proud of me." This may sound a bit braggadocious, but that's the point. Take time to brag about the amazing job you're doing by staying committed to your routine, because it matters. Give yourself a pat on the back and a round of applause every single time you do your routine. You deserve it.

Celebrate the Result

I don't know about you, but I love seeing the results of my actions and the outcome from my routines. This in itself is a reward. If you find yourself struggling to keep your routine going, focus on the result you'll get from completing your routine. Will your home or environment look more appealing? Will you feel less stressed and more prepared? You may not always want to do the action steps within your routine, but you will typically still want the result that stem from it. Focusing on the result can be strong enough to spring you into action. Keep this in mind as you strive to remain consistent with your routine.

Never underestimate the power of rewards. They can help you build the momentum needed to turn your routine into a habitual flow. If you love a challenge, this tool could be a game changer for you. Think about this now. In which ways can you reward yourself after completing your routine? Which rewards resonate most with you? Give it a try, you just may notice your consistency improve.

Products and Resources

Can I share a secret with you? I love a good notepad, planner, or checklist to keep me on the right track. I've used a variety of products over the years to help me remain consistent with my goals, so when routines became a staple in my life, I knew I needed products and resources to help me remain committed.

Products for your routine are similar to reminders because they can prompt you to get and keep your routine going. However, the wrong one can steer you off course. Be sure the product you invest in is as specific as possible to helping you carry out routines consistently.

A routine tracker is a specific product that can impact your ability to maintain your routine, especially if you tend to be motivated by accomplishment. Tracking your progress includes making a physical note, such as a checkmark, next to the date and/or time the routine is completed. This visual representation of accomplishment creates confidence and momentum for keeping the routine going.

Tracking your progress is a powerful tool because it serves as both a reminder and reward. You're reminded by the product itself and your reward is the accomplishment of doing the routine you set out to do. This, together, can cause steady traction with your routine.

Along with products, resources can also assist you with maintaining your routine. Resources include educational materials and the help of others. For those times when you may need a helping hand, businesses and services can carry out your routine for you. As a personal example, I enjoy having someone else take care of my weekly grocery shopping and ship my monthly cleaning supplies to my door. Using these resources has saved me time, energy, and money as well as kept my routines thriving. You don't have to do it all. Rely on products and resources to help you remain in flow with your routine.

The **ROUTINE BUILDING** Handbook

Teisha's Routine-Building Story

Problem: Teisha was struggling to stay organized while juggling work and two businesses. She had the belief that she couldn't stay organized with everything on her plate.

What helped: Teisha purchased the Routine and Things Daily Planning Notepad as a gift to herself. The notepad includes an area for mindfulness, with prompts like "I'm feeling," "I'm grateful for," and "My intention for today is." The notepad is also geared toward maintaining focus and clarity by having a brain dump area, room to write down top three daily goals, and space to map out the schedule for the day.

Outcome: Teisha finally found a planning product that helped her stay organized and able to manage the many facets of her life. The breakdown of mindfulness, clarity, and focus has helped her stay on track with her calendar, and she is excelling at work and business.

"When I first got the Routine and Things Daily Planning Notepad, I didn't know that it would change my life. I always thought I couldn't be organized. It always took me longer than most to grasp concepts and lessons. I would easily get frustrated because I couldn't stay organized. When I saw this planning pad, I thought to myself, 'why not, let me try.' I have used it every day since. This planning pad gave me confidence in learning and staying on track with my calendar. I work full-time and own two businesses, so being organized is essential to my success. I don't know how Ashley made a planning pad so perfect, but I feel like she made it just for me!"

Products and Resources by Category

The table below shares a variety of products and resources specific to the five routine categories mentioned in Chapter 1. Each product and resource can help you remain more consistent with your routine. Remember, the more aligned the product is with your routine, the better outcome you'll have.

To grab many of the products and resources below, visit routineandthings.com.

Cooking	Cleaning	Children	Planning	Self-Care
Meal-Planning Notepad	Weekly Cleaning Notepad	Weekly Children Notepad	Daily Planner

Weekly Planner | Journal

Affirmations |
| Recipe Bank

Weekly Meal List | Cleaning Checklist

Cleaning Product Delivery Service | Chore Cards

Routine Cards | Monthly Planner

Work Checklist | Self-Care Monthly Subscription Box |
| Food Subscription Service | | School Checklist | | Brain Dump Notepad |
| Grocery Delivery Service | Cleaning Supplies and Tools | Books about Routines | Travel Checklist

Family Planner | Self-Care Door Hanger |
| Grocery Pickup | Laundry Service | Daily Routine Checklist | | Exercise Program |

The more tools you intentionally use to keep your routine on track, the more success you'll achieve. It's time to fill your toolbox by understanding which tools are most impactful for you and your routine. Keep your routine at the top of your mind in a variety of ways, reward yourself often for your consistency, and use products and resources that can assist you along the way. On those days when maintaining your routine is more challenging, you'll have more than enough assistance to stay in flow.

Chapter 9
MAINTENANCE FAQS

Maintaining a routine is where many struggle, but no longer will this be your story. Below are answers to the most frequently asked questions for adhering to any routine. Take your time with this chapter because the key to consistently reaping the benefits of your routine lies in your ability to maintain it.

Q: Is it possible to maintain a routine?

A: It is absolutely possible to stick to a routine. When you create a manageable routine that aligns with your life, you will have more success maintaining it. Yes, there will be days you skip or miss your routine, but maintenance is less about doing your routine daily and more about your ability to start again. Give yourself time to adjust to a new routine and eliminate the need for perfection. Your routine is more sustainable when you release the pressure to succeed.

Q: What are some top tips for staying consistent with routines?

A: Tip 1: When you notice you're struggling to maintain consistency, determine the root cause and do your best to eliminate the roadblock.

Tip 2: Be kind to yourself throughout the process and release the need to have a perfect routine.

Tip 3: Make your routines as fun and flexible as they can be.

Tip 4: Use a variety of tools to stay on track.

Tip 5: Seek help when you need it. Learning to maintain your routine doesn't have to fall entirely on your shoulders.

Q: I struggle to maintain routines. Can anything help?

A: I can offer a range of suggestions, but start with figuring out the root cause of your roadblock or struggle. It's possible you may have a mental block keeping you stuck. Mental roadblocks often occur when expectations aren't managed. Thinking in all-or-nothing terms, taking your routines too seriously, and not being kind to yourself in the process are all roadblocks that can cause you to struggle with maintaining your routines.

On the other hand, other types of roadblocks could be hindering your progress. Common roadblocks include time conflicts, tiredness, routine fatigue, and sabotaging behaviors. There are some remedies that can steer you back on course. Chapter 7 dives into recognizing your resistance. This chapter will help you get back on track and give you the momentum you need to stick with your routine. Once you are aware of what's causing friction with your routine, you can make an informed decision that will help you overcome the struggle to maintain it.

Q: How do I get back into a routine after not doing it for a while?

A: When you've gotten behind on your routine, the key is to simply start again. Here are three things that can help you do so:

1. Be kind to yourself after falling behind and give yourself permission to start again. It can feel uncomfortable to miss days or weeks of your routine, but if you criticize yourself this will likely keep you stuck in inaction. Instead, be kind and graciously allow yourself to start again.

2. Understand why you have fallen behind. Without knowing what caused you to repeatedly miss your routine, the cycle will continue. Uncover the root cause of your missed routine and identify ways to address and eliminate the problem.

3. Do the routine. Momentum comes with movement, so starting the routine again will give you the energetic wind to keep going. Falling behind on your routine doesn't equal failure. Things happen and life can get crazy, but when you make the choice to start again, you are saying yes to living the abundant life you want and deserve.

Q: What are common roadblocks that can throw me off track, and how do I overcome them?

A: Common roadblocks include feeling tired, time conflicts, routine fatigue, and distractions. More than likely you will face one if not all while maintaining your routine. You can avoid most of these roadblocks if you are proactive and take action in advance, but in some cases, avoiding these roadblocks may not be possible. If a roadblock does present itself, quickly identify it and brainstorm ways to move beyond it. If you notice that a roadblock is constantly showing up, this could be a sign to revamp your routine or create a different routine that will address the recurring issue. In Chapter 8

I fully discuss common roadblocks faced when adhering to routines and offer suggestions for ways to overcome them.

Q: I'm often tired. How can I stay consistent when I'm constantly fatigued?

A: Low energy will dramatically impact your consistency and momentum, so discovering the root cause is the first step. There are different types of tiredness, which means your approach and remedy for each will be different. Possibly, you're physically tired because you constantly go to bed late, or maybe you're mentally fatigued because your job drains you. Below are some questions you can ask yourself to uncover what's causing your fatigue. Once you're more aware of the issue, you can put parameters in place to help. Questions to ask yourself (feel free to write the answers in the lines provided):

- Am I physically, mentally, or emotionally tired?

  ....

- What's causing me to constantly be tired? Do I recognize any patterns?

  ....

  ....

  ....

- What's one thing I can do today or this week that can help me feel more rested and energized?

  ....

  ....

  ....

FYI: If work is the source of your constant fatigue, quitting your job may not be an option. Is there a way to shift your perspective or increase your self-care to alleviate the physical, mental or emotional overload?

Q: Instead of doing my routine, I often find myself doing something else. What can help me stay focused?

A: To stay focused on your routine, I suggest that you start with setting boundaries and getting clear on your sabotaging behaviors. Boundaries help you know what is within limits and when you're going outside the limits. When you plan to do your routine, you are setting a boundary with yourself, so anything that falls outside of this, unless urgent, can be done at another time.

Boundaries only work if you uphold them. Consider which routine boundaries you are not willing to cross and put them in place. Knowing the ways you unintentionally sabotage your progress will get you back on track as well. We tend to find comfort in taking the easier road, so when you find yourself doing another thing instead of committing to your routine, this is a sign of sabotaging behavior. Self-sabotage is sneaky and can show up in a variety of ways. Get familiar with your sabotaging behaviors, call them out, and stay the course.

Q: Should I do my routine daily to strengthen consistency?

A: Yes, daily routines can help strengthen your consistency, but it isn't required or necessary. Doing a routine a few days a week or once a week will also strengthen your consistency. Determine how often you need this routine in your life and commit to sticking to that schedule. A manageable routine schedule is what actually strengthens consistency.

Q: I'm juggling many routines. How can I manage them all at once?

A: When juggling multiple routines, consider these tips:

Keep Your Routines Simple

Is there space for you to simplify your routines? If so, this is a great place to start. Remove actions that aren't needed or eliminate a step that is complicating your routine.

Distribute Your Routines Appropriately

It can be very hard to manage a bunch of routines at once. Consider appropriately assigning your routines to daily, weekly, or monthly time frames, making sure to disperse the routines evenly. For example, if there is a daily routine you can easily turn into a weekly routine to offload your day, try doing so. This could look like doing laundry on the weekends instead of doing a load every day. This will alleviate daily stress and create more balance in your life. It is also helpful to consider how much time and energy you have available before committing to multiple routines at once.

Maintain Necessary Routines

Although routines are great, there's no need to crowd your life with them. Only maintain those that are truly important for you to thrive. Once you can smoothly manage the most important routines, then you can begin to add on more. I personally find having a few staple routines is all that's needed to keep me grounded and at ease.

Q: Is it helpful to track my progress?

A: Tracking your progress is an extremely helpful method for remaining consistent with your routine. You get instant gratification when you physically check off the completion of your routine. Plus seeing your progress over time can be an amazing motivating factor to keep you headed in the right direction. Paying attention to your progress can be very rewarding, but do not allow your progress to define who you are or validate your worthiness. I suggest that you focus on your commitment and growth instead of your productivity.

Q: Which tools can help me stay consistent with my routine?

A: Use reminders to help with sticking to your routine and rewards as a catalyst to propel you when challenges arise. Even specific products can serve as motivators. Knowing what works for you is key. Chapter 8 dives into each of these tools in depth and offers more information so you can make the best choice when deciding which tools are right for you.

Q: Are there any specific products that are best for maintaining routines?

A: When the product directly aligns with the routine, it's much easier for it to help you carry out the actions in your routine. For example, if you start an exercise routine, an exercise app could be a great product for maintaining your routine. Your products are only as good as your intent to use them, so avoid becoming a product junkie and select products you'll actually use. Chapter 8 shares a list of specific products for different routine categories. Take a look at the list for product inspiration. There are also plenty of amazing routine-inspired products at routineandthings.com.

Q: How can I best remember my routines?

A: One of the most successful ways to remember your routine is to record it somewhere. This can include writing it down on a sheet of paper or typing it out electronically on your phone or computer. Once you start a new routine, it can be difficult to recall it without a reference. Record your routine and place it in a designated area so you can easily refer to it when needed.

Another effective way to remember your routine is to keep in mind your Easy Yes. This is the main reason routine is valuable for your life. Your Easy Yes is a great reminder for staying on course. Chapter 1 goes into detail about how to determine your Easy Yes and provides some useful examples.

Q: Can you share how you personally maintain your routines?

A: I've had a lot of practice with creating routines over the years, and I've noticed a few things help:

- Keeping my routines simple
  I try to keep my routines to five steps or less. I've found this increases my likelihood of sticking with the routine. My rule of thumb is, if I can't easily recall the routine, then it's not simple enough.

- Doing my routines at an optimal time
  When deciding where to place my routines in my life, I assess my daily and weekly schedules. I choose a time during the day or week that works best for my current lifestyle. For example, when I was a stay-at-home mom, I chose to do the kitchen routine in the morning because I had enough time and energy to commit to maintaining it.

- Prioritizing my routines
  I prioritize maintaining routines that are absolutely necessary for my day-to-day to run smoothly. Having too many routines can cause overwhelm and decrease the joy that comes with a degree of spontaneity. I choose to prioritize routines that are in direct alignment with what matters most to me.

- Having fun with my routines!

  Fun is nonnegotiable and must be included in my routines. This is usually anything from listening to a podcast as I clean the kitchen or tuning in to a relaxing meditation before bed. I ensure enjoyment is baked into my routine because this has made a dramatic improvement on my ability to maintain it.

These four things tremendously help to keep my routines going. As you are adopting routines into your life, pay attention to what helps your routine thrive and continue to do those things. Little by little, you will understand what best helps you maintain your routines.

Part 4
FOR MAMAS

Chapter 10
ROUTINES AND MOTHERHOOD

As a woman who struggled in her role as a stay-at-home mom, I knew this book needed a chapter specifically for women navigating motherhood. Although many factors influenced the hot mess of my life during that time, I strongly believe if I had a foundation of healthy routines, I would not have experienced as much difficulty. Routines were my saving grace. I'm sharing what I know in hopes that you can move beyond survival mode or avoid the struggle that I experienced.

As you may know, there's a huge difference between managing routines for yourself and managing routines for an entire family. Building routines when children are involved can be challenging for sure. This chapter is for the new mom transitioning into unknown territory, for the experienced mom who needs a bit of help getting back on track, for the mom who's burned out and looking for restoration, and for the mom who seems to have it all together but is silently suffering day after day. May you find clarity, ease, and happiness.

Children and Family

"Have kids," they said. "It will be cute," they said. Until you realize you're responsible for an entire human being that interrupts you any time you're doing something important, always needs a snack, and never seems to be satisfied. Then there's routine. Any pediatrician will tell you routine is important for children. As Dr. Katie Penry, author of *The Parenting Toddlers Workbook* says, behavioral routines are routines that are so regular and so consistent that they become habitual and influential for the rest of your child's life Although a bit daunting at times, creating and maintaining routines for your children and family can be much simpler than you think. Take a look at the questions and answers below to get started.

Q: What's the best way to go about creating routines for small children?

A: When creating routines for your small children, you can apply the same routine-building process you use for your own life. However, take your child and their natural tendencies and flow into account. Often, we restrict our children with super-rigid routines that box them into a way of living that feels uncomfortable. This will usually show up as rebellion or resistance to the routine you've created for them. To avoid this, be sure to create flexible routines so your child can experience the comfort in routine. Also, because every child is different, flexible routines help greatly when there is more than one child involved. Start with identifying the routine your child needs and keep simplicity, realistic expectations, flexibility, and fun in mind. See examples below.

- **Simplicity:** Create a routine chart with your child, making it simple for both of you to recall and follow.

- **Realistic expectations:** If your child is always hungry after school, instead of their after-school routine beginning with homework, begin with a small snack instead.

- **Flexibility:** If you are too tired to read a book during your child's bedtime routine, have the child read the book or give the child the book to flip through as you rest your head for 10 minutes.

- **Fun:** A fun way to make getting out the door and to school on time easier is to reward the child with a movie night at the end of the week for sticking to the routine.

Q: Which routines are important for toddlers/preschoolers?

A: This is totally up to you. Each child is different, and the most important routine for them will depend upon what they need in their season of life. Think about which area of your child's day feels chaotic, where constant challenge exists, or where you would like to invite in more structure. In our family, our children maintain morning and bedtime routines that welcome security and structure day after day. Below are some children's routines for you to consider but remember to only create and start one at a time. This will ensure a smoother transition for not only your kids but for you as well.

⇨ Morning Routine

Suggested steps: Make bed, brush teeth, wash face, get dressed

Frequency: Daily (upon wake-up)

Timing: ~ 20 minutes

Purpose: For your child to get ready for the day ahead

⇨ Bedtime Routine

Suggested steps: Bath, pajamas, book time, prayer

Frequency: Daily before bed

Timing: ~ 45 minutes

Purpose: To settle child so they sleep well

⇨ Homeschool Routine

Suggested steps: Learning time, subject activity, lunch, reading, craft activity

Frequency: Five days a week (homeschooling days)

Timing: ~ 6 hours

Purpose: To stay on schedule with learning and development

⇨ After-School Routine

Suggested Steps: Snack, homework, playtime

Frequency: 5 days a week after school

Timing: ~ 2 hours

Purpose: To direct child on what to do after school

⇨ Nap Routine

Suggested Steps: White noise, lights out, naptime

Frequency: Daily after lunchtime

Timing: ~ 2 to 3 hours

Purpose: To alleviate tantrums from overtiredness

⇨ Learning Routine

Suggested steps: Reading, flash cards, craft activity

Frequency: 3 days a week in the morning after breakfast

Timing: ~ 2.5 hours

Purpose: To promote learning for toddler

⇨ Weekend Routine

Suggested steps: Breakfast, playtime, walk outside, TV time

Frequency: Weekend days (Saturday, Sunday) in the morning

Timing: ~ 3.5 hours

Purpose: To have more structure on the weekends so children stay preoccupied and engaged

Q: How do I get my children on board with new routines?

A: Communication and collaboration are key. If your children are old enough to give input on their routine, collaborate with them during the creation process. They will feel more connected to the routine and more likely to have success with maintaining it.

When it comes to quick shifts in routine due to a temporary change in schedule, communication with your child about the change is a must. Proactively prepare your child for the change in routine.

This helps them understand what to expect and helps to ease the transition to the new change. For example, if your child is starting preschool for the first time, talk with them about how they will have to wake up earlier and that morning TV time will need to be shorter in order to get to school on time. Without communication, your child is likely to experience frustration or discomfort, which usually shows up as tantrums and unruly behavior. Collaborate with your child by giving them choices on what they can do instead and allow them to make the decision. Giving them a sense of control will help them feel safe again. Change causes feelings of unease and uncertainty, but with communication and collaboration, your child is likely to get on board with their new routine.

Q: How can I get my children involved in cleaning routines for the home?

A: If you want to get your children involved with cleaning the home, kudos to you. I believe everyone in a home has a responsibility to help keep it clean and tidy because everyone contributes to the mess. If your children are at the age where they can be directed to clean or cleaning can become an autonomous chore, you can collaborate with them to build new cleaning routines that they are in charge of. Work with them to build a routine that teaches them the process of creating routines as well as allow them to have input in how they would like to clean.

For smaller children, you can decide which routines are best suited for their age and instruct them to help with a certain routine. I find that cleaning routines such as tidying and helping with dish washing are great for smaller kids. For more autonomous children, it can be wise to ask which cleaning routine they would like to take part in. Cleaning routines for older kids can include kitchen tasks, mopping, laundry, and taking out trash. Of course if your child is having difficulty deciding, remain patient but also set a firm boundary for when the decision is needed so that they don't get off the hook with helping to clean the home. Time to get excited, because help is coming!

Q: With children, how can I lessen interruptions in my routines?

A: As you are well aware, interruptions are going to happen, especially when children are involved. I honestly wish our kids had a barometer to know when not to interrupt. Unfortunately, this isn't the case, and for this reason, we have to make adjustments as parents. Luckily, there are a few things you can try to help lessen interruptions in your routines.

1. If possible, do the routine when the children aren't around. You can do the routine while the kids are at school, when the grandparents volunteer to care for them, or when they are asleep. Yes, this will mean you may not have time to binge Netflix child-free, but at least you can focus and get the routine done in a timely manner.

2. Anticipate the interruptions and plan for them. As moms, we can usually anticipate our child's needs. When you are planning to do a routine with your child nearby, think about what they will need during that time and set them up to have what they need in advance. For example, when I do our kitchen routine, I will put on an educational TV show and give my children a snack. This usually keeps their attention long enough for me to do the entire routine without much interruption.

3. Get your child involved. If your child is old enough and the routine is something they can assist with, this is a win-win for you.

Not only will your child be too preoccupied to interrupt you, you will also get help with the routine.

Q: How do I help my teenage children create their own routines?

A: To help your teenagers create routines of their own, first, help them identify the routine most important for their life at this moment. Try not to decide this for them unless they ask for your opinion. Your child can think about where they would like to see improvement in their own life or where they are experiencing the most discomfort.

If your teenager will soon be entering adulthood and leaving home, it can be helpful to start a routine in an area where they lack maturity or skill. For example, maybe your teenager can improve their cleaning or communication skills because expertise in these areas will serve them well as they become more independent. The most important factor in helping your teen create routines is to allow them to take the lead as much as possible. This will strengthen their ability to build routines, which will come in handy as they progress through life.

Q: Which routines are specifically important for teenagers?

A: This depends on which routines will best support the teen in strengthening their independence. Routines related to hygiene, cleanliness, communication, emotional regulation, and self-care are great places to start. Be sure to allow your teenager to lead the routine-building process while you offer guidance when needed. Below is a list of routines that may be helpful for your teen to consider when deciding which routine is best for them.

⇨ Skin-Care Routine

Suggested steps: Wash face > apply serum > apply moisturizer

Timing: 10 minutes

Purpose: Helps teen with caring for skin daily (especially if they deal with acne and breakouts)

⇨ Hair-Care Routine

Suggested steps: Wash hair > condition hair > apply moisturizer > style as desired

Timing: Depends on hair type and texture

Purpose: Helps teen with washing and styling their hair on their own

⇨ Bathroom-Cleaning Routine

Suggested steps: Clean sink, toilet, and tub > sweep floor > wipe mirror

Timing: about 30 minutes

Purpose: Helps teen with becoming comfortable with cleaning the bathroom appropriately

⇨ Kitchen Routine

Suggested steps: Wash dishes > wipe down countertops and stove > sweep floor if needed

Timing: about 30 minutes

Purpose: Helps teen with learning how to keep a kitchen clean and tidy

⇨ Meal-Prep Routine

Suggested steps: Find recipe > cook meal > package meal

Timing: about 1 hour

Purpose: Helps teen with preparing meals in advance to promote preparedness

⇨ Morning Routine

Suggested steps: Gratitude practice > shower > journal

Timing: about 30 minutes

Purpose: Helps teen to understand self-care is important first thing in the morning

⇨ Bedtime Routine

Suggested steps: Shower > phone away > meditate

Timing: about 30 minutes

Purpose: Helps teen get to bed at an ideal time and sleep better

⇨ Exercise Routine

Suggested steps: Stretch > exercise > drink glass of water

Timing: about 45 minutes

Purpose: Helps teen keep their physical health a priority

⇨ Meditation Routine

Suggested steps: Choose meditation > find comfortable position > meditate

Timing: Depends on length of meditation

Purpose: Helps teen connect with their inner truth or lessen anxiety and overwhelm

⇨ Critical Thinking Routine

Suggested steps: Assess current situation > ask clarifying questions > make decision on how to proceed

Timing: Depends on how challenging the situation is

Purpose: Helps teen learn to problem solve without your assistance

⇨ Emergency Routine

Suggested steps: Take a deep breath > call 911 > call us (parents) if possible

Timing: Depends on the emergency

Purpose: Helps teen respond to an emergency situation when you are not around

Q: How can I incorporate family time into routine?

A: The easiest way to incorporate family time into routine is to get everyone in the household involved. Making a few of your home routines a family affair can give you all more time with each other. Routines such as setting the table for dinner, cleaning the kitchen, or tidying the home can be awesome for communication and being present with the family. You can also think about creating a new routine specifically for family time. This could look like having a family movie night every Friday, bike-riding every Saturday morning, or engaging in conversation during dinner each night.

Create a routine that works for your family and be sure to make it enjoyable for everyone involved.

Q: What are some ways to encourage my significant other to take part in routines?

A: Getting your significant other to jump on the routine band-wagon can take time, and there's no guarantee they will get on board. Your best shot is through your approach. Take into account these three considerations:

1. Communicate why having a routine is important to you and why you want it to be a part of your life together. Our partners love to make us happy. When you express the importance routines have on your happiness, many times this will cause them to take action.

2. Communicate how the routine will benefit your partner. Usually, if your partner understands the benefit the routine will have on their life, they are more likely to give it a try. Talk with your partner about specific ways the routine will bring value to their day-to-day. Help them understand how having a certain routine aligns with their goals in life. This is a really great catalyst for peaking their interest.

3. Manage your expectations. When approaching the conversation, your significant other will either decide to get on board or be hesitant to adopt the routine. If the latter happens, remain patient and be the example. Once your partner sees you are thriving by having this routine, they may decide to get in line. You can also revisit the conversation at a later date if it is a routine you need your partner to support you with.

You may want to start an exercise routine with your partner but they are a bit hesitant. Speak about how moving your body has helped to increase your energy and focus, and share how intimacy and sex improves with exercise. After hearing how both of you will benefit, I'm pretty sure your partner would be happy to start the routine.

To hear more ways to get your partner on board with routines, listen to episodes 030 and 052 of the *Routine and Things* podcast. Check out the resources section of this book for the link to the podcast.

Q: What can help me become more present with my kids and family?

A: As a mom, being present at all times can be a challenge. With plenty to do and much on your mind, remaining present comes with practice. Below are a couple of routines I've found helpful for engaging in the present moment.

1. Gratitude Practice: To be present in any moment, start by expressing gratitude for what is happening at that moment. Ask yourself, "What am I grateful for right now?" This can help to get you out of your head and into the experience you want to engage in.

2. Experiencing the Five Senses: When you find yourself disconnecting from the present moment, stop and explore your five senses in the moment. Ask yourself,

- What do I see?
- What do I hear?
- What do I feel?
- What do I smell?
- What can I taste?

Doing this simple routine reengages you in the present moment and allows you to have a more profound experience.

When it comes to remaining present, you're not alone. Begin to put these routines into practice and soak up any and every moment you can.

Najah's Routine-Building Story

Problem: Najah was returning to work after a long break as a stay-at-home mom. She needed help with managing the transition so she didn't lose sight of herself or her home.

What helped: Najah is a regular listener of the *Routine and Things* podcast, and one episode in particular (episode 39) helped her create and start an ideal morning routine for her life. In the episode I talk about what helps you rock your routines. I shared how mindset is a huge barrier to routine building, routines do not have to be done daily, and it's best to keep them simple. They are created to support your specific life so you will have much more success.

Outcome: Najah started a morning routine consisting of getting coffee or tea and alone time with a book before the kids woke up. This helped her start her mornings feeling productive and at ease. After experiencing the amazing benefits of her morning routine, this fueled her to create and start more routines for her home. Her transition to back to work was a lot smoother than she could have imagined.

"When I decided to go back to work to support my family, establishing a routine was the answer I never knew I needed.

It started with a morning routine, and the results were not only immediate but so effective that I began to put routines in place for every area of my life. My husband and I have two boys ages three and one; my oldest is autistic and comes with a schedule of his own packed with therapies and development classes. I didn't realize how much I was relying on remembering things in my head and going day to day, barely making it with my kids, and I knew I needed something solid in place to help me manage a career and my home. Before I had no time for myself to implement self-care or work out after a long day. I am extremely grateful for finding Ashley and her life-changing routine strategies. My kids have better morning and evening routines. I have now made room for my passions and interests outside of work and have experienced a huge shift in my mood and productivity. I am able to work full time without feeling like I'm drowning in a never-ending to do list. The results from establishing a routine are extremely addictive and worth putting in the work."

Transition and Change

Change is constant, even more so for moms. Just when you get used to a certain routine, here comes change. Transition is something we moms have to become comfortable with, because if not, we are more likely to experience difficulty along the journey.

To adjust to change within routines, you must first understand that change is inevitable. Your routines will shift constantly during the span of your life and your family's life. Once you accept this truth, you will move toward finding solutions that will help make transitions easier to manage. Below are questions and answers for navigating change within routine.

Q: My family and I are moving. Is it best to keep the routines I have?

Assess how your day-to-day will be impacted by the transition. Doing this will help you determine whether or not to keep the routines you have in place. If the transition can't handle your current routines, consider revamping your routine or creating a brand-new one. In my experience, there's usually no need for a complete overhaul of your routines but instead small tweaks as you adjust to your new transition. Here are some questions to help you decide between keeping the routines you have versus bringing in new ones.

- Will my new environment support my current routines?

  ....

  ....

- Is this an emotional transition, and do I have routines to help?

  ....

  ....

- What will be different in my day-to-day?

  ....

  ....

- Do I see my current routines fitting into my new lifestyle?

  ....

  ....

- What adjustments can I make to my routines to accommodate the transition?

....

....

Q: As a new mom, how can I easily establish a morning routine?

A: Establishing a morning routine as a new mom can be challenging. With the shift in your hormones, adjusting to your new role, and caring for a little human around the clock, naturally your morning will look different. Over time, you will begin to develop a natural routine as you continue to bond with your new bundle of joy. However, if you want to be proactive and take intentional action toward getting into a morning routine, you can consider the following (feel free to jot down notes in the lines provided):

- Your baby's sleep schedule: What time does your baby usually wake up in the morning. Do they go back to sleep after feeding or stay awake for a few hours? If your baby goes back to sleep, this could be a window of opportunity to do a small morning routine that starts your day off in a beautiful way.

....

....

- Your sleep schedule: How much sleep are you getting each night? If you are only getting a small amount and feel exhausted when you wake up, consider holding off on a morning routine. It's more important you get the rest you need.

....

....

- Your baby's feeding schedule: Take this into consideration when creating a morning routine. Usually, babies like to eat as soon as they wake up. If you're planning to do your morning routine before baby wakes up, give yourself enough time for the routine so it lessens your chance of being interrupted.

  ....

  ....

- Your physical ability: Maybe you want to add exercise to your morning routine. Be sure you are physically able to move your body in the way you desire before considering this action. You may not be ready for a full HIIT workout but a good morning stretch will do you just as good.

  ....

  ....

- Your emotional health: How are you feeling emotionally? If you feel that your emotional health could be stronger, consider adding mindfulness activities like journaling and gratitude practice to your morning routine. Lack of sleep leads to a weakened emotional state so if you are not sleeping enough, try not to rush into a morning routine at this time.

  ....

  ....

These considerations will help you understand how a morning routine can fit into your life, plus which actions in the routine are best for you to focus on. I recommend not rushing into routine as a new mom. The added pressure can negatively affect your emotional health. Practice managing your expectations because things will look and feel a lot different. Take your time adjusting to motherhood, and a routine will naturally begin to fall into place.

Once you've adjusted to the transition and are feeling comfortable in your new role, then you can begin creating a more structured and intentional morning.

Q: I recently had a baby and am interested in some simple routines to maintain self-care and to bond with my baby. Any ideas?

A: Your emotional and physical health along with your attachment to your new child are most important. Keep the routines simple, flexible, and fun and they will have an amazing impact for you and your new baby. For inspiration, a few routines are listed below, including a simple Mommy and Me morning routine.

⇨ Mommy and Me Morning Routine

Suggested steps: Feed baby > Practice gratitude (say three thing you're grateful for) > Move body

Frequency: Each morning

Timing: ~ 1 hour

Purpose: To bond with baby and focus on mental and physical health first thing in the morning

⇨ Bedtime Routine

Suggested steps: Mommy shower > Baby bath> Feeding > White noise > Lights out

Frequency: Each day at bedtime

Timing: ~ 2 hours

Purpose: To help you and baby create a calm environment before bed, which promotes better sleep for you both

⇨ **Movement Routine**

Suggested steps: Stretch > Go for a walk

Frequency: 3 to 5 days a week after baby's first nap

Timing: ~ 45 minutes

Purpose: To increase physical activity and get outside with baby

⇨ **Feeding Routine**

Suggested steps: Get in comfortable position > Feed baby > Burp baby

Frequency: With each feeding

Timing: ~ 1 hour

Purpose: To promote comfort for you and baby during feedings

Q: I'm transitioning to be a stay-at-home mom. Which routines will help support my day-to-day?

A: It's important to take your lifestyle and responsibilities into account before deciding which routines are best for you. However, here are some specific routines that helped me thrive as a stay-at-home mom. You will notice that many routines are listed, but remember I didn't start them all at once. I suggest that you start one routine at a time. With time, you will begin to build a unique web of routines specific for your lifestyle and responsibilities.

Self-Care Routines (morning and bedtime)

⇨ **Morning Routine**

Steps: Prayer > State how I am feeling > Gratitude practice

Frequency: Each morning

Timing: ~ 15 minutes

Purpose: To start my morning with mindfulness

⇨ **Bedtime Routine**

Steps: Shower > Journal > Prayer > Meditation

Frequency: Each night before bed

Timing: ~ 1 hour

Purpose: To help me fall asleep quicker and sleep better

Cleaning Routines

⇨ **Laundry**

Steps: Wash laundry > Fold laundry > Put laundry away

Frequency: Weekly in one day

Timing: ~ 8 hours (usually the entire day)

Purpose: To keep up with laundry and get it done in a day

⇨ **Tidy**

Steps: Pick up items off floor > Clean dining room table > Sweep

Frequency: Every evening before bed

Timing: ~ 20 minutes

Purpose: To decrease anxiety and ensure I woke up to a tidy home

Cooking Routine

⇨ Meal Planning

Steps: Take an inventory of what I have > Choose weekly meals > Go grocery shopping

Frequency: Weekly on Sunday

Timing: ~ 2 hours (including grocery shopping)

Purpose: To feel prepared for the week so I'm not scrambling to figure out dinner at the last minute

Children Routine

⇨ Morning

Steps: Wash face > Brush teeth > Get dressed > Breakfast

Frequency: Each morning

Timing: ~ 45 minutes

Purpose: To start the morning knowing what to expect

⇨ Bedtime

Steps: Bath > Book > Prayer > Lights out

Frequency: Each night

Timing: ~ 1 hour

Purpose: To ease my children into bed

⇨ Learning

Steps: Flash cards > Reading

Frequency: 3 times a week after breakfast

Timing: ~ 30 minutes

Purpose: To give us something to do in the morning and help with child's development

⇨ Weekly Planning

Steps: Brain dump > Decide top 3 priorities > Assign 3 additional tasks for each day

Frequency: Weekly on Sunday

Timing: ~ 30 minutes

Purpose: To prepare for the week ahead

Q: There's a new child in the family. How can I stick to our current routines?

A: Luckily , a new child won't dramatically affect most routines. Yes, your workload will increase but the actions usually remain the same. For example, the amount of laundry and dishes will increase but there wouldn't be a need for the laundry and dishwashing routines to change. These factors allow you to adhere to routines even when another child comes into the fold.

Although some routines will not be impacted, others may shift as a result of a new child. For example, you may not be able to do your morning jog now that the new baby is affecting your sleep schedule, or the daily routine for your children may need to be adjusted to accommodate the child's feeding schedule. You will need to consider the new child's temperament, natural rhythm, and needs. It may be tempting to proactively change the routine but instead of rushing to revamp or create a new routine, it is best to wait until you have a better understanding of what changes need to be made. Do you now need to change your children's playdate time because of the new child's nap schedule? Possibly you need to revamp your evening routine to include getting the baby bottles prepped for the next day. All in all, when welcoming a new child to the family, remain patient, stick to the routines you have, and wait to see how your routines will change, if at all.

Q: Our schedule changes often. How can I maintain an exercise routine when our days are unpredictable?

A: This is the beauty of routines. Routines have the ability to stay the same even when your days feel all over the place. It is possible to maintain an exercise routine with an unpredictable schedule and here's how.

Get comfortable with moving your routine around. Determine the time of day and place your exercise routine fits best into your typical schedule. Maybe mornings at home before the kids wake up work best for you because most days you typically start work at 3 p.m. However, on the days where you start work at 7 a.m., you can move your workout to the evenings. Exercise can be done whenever and wherever, which means you don't have to skip it just because your schedule changes. When your schedule changes, change when and where you do the routine, and this will help to keep you on track with exercising.

Q: Is it okay to create seasonal, or temporary routines?

A: It is totally normal to create seasonal routines, especially if this is an intentional decision. Routines are created and maintained to support your current lifestyle. When your lifestyle shifts, new people are added to the family, or you change as an individual, your routines are likely to change as well. Routines are not meant to last forever. Focus on what your routine can do for your life at this moment and when you notice the routine has run its course, you can adopt a new one.

When my daughters were not in school, I would do a morning routine with them, but once they started attending school, this routine was no longer needed. I've also switched out my morning routines multiple times throughout the year, depending on what I need most at the time. For a few months, I had a morning routine that included mindfulness activities such as journaling and gratitude practice, but now my morning routine consists of drinking warm water and exercise. Seasons will change, and the season you're in now may not look the same a week, month, or year from now. Embracing that routines may only serve you temporarily is a healthy perspective to have and can create more ease during the routine-building process.

Ariana's Routine-Building Story

Problem: Ariana was feeling nervous about the transition from one child to two. She was already winging it, which was causing her immense stress. With juggling a business, work, and school, she didn't know how she would manage it all with grace and ease.

What helped: Ariana listened to a couple of episodes of the *Routine and Things* podcast and realized routines could be created on her terms. Instead of building routines that felt like she was a drill sergeant at home, she leaned into creating flexible routines to support her unique needs

Outcome: Ariana bought the Routine and Things Daily Planning Notepad and decided to build a planning routine.

Ariana now feels in flow and can better manage the things on her plate with intention and ease. She and her family are thriving and she is prioritizing her health and well-being every day.

"The first time I found Ashley and Routine and Things, I found my sanity. I started listening to Routine and Things podcast at a pivotal moment in my life after having my second child. I was nervous about what life would look like juggling two kids, a business, work, and school. Ashley has a way of sharing practical routine habits that don't make me feel like a robot checking off a to-do list. I went from a stressed-out mom winging it, who believed this is how life is supposed to be, to a woman who is present and confidently conquers all things with peace of mind. I can't thank Ashley enough for what she does."

Self-Love and Self-Care

As a mom, have you found it's easier to create routines for your family than creating them for yourself? If you answered yes, you're not alone. It's understandable to focus on our children more than ourselves because, historically, sacrifice and martyrdom in motherhood has been praised. It's a new age and no longer necessary or customary to lose sight of yourself in order to prove you're a good mom. You have the power to build nourishing routines for yourself that fill you with joy, gratitude, and love. Each question and answer below will help you make this happen.

Q: Is there a specific self-care routine I need as a mom?

A: To care for yourself is to care for those around you. Placing your self-care on the backburner isn't helpful for anyone, including you. There's no specific routine that will be best for you as a mom; the routine you choose to build depends upon your specific needs at the moment. Below are some points to create your self-care routine on your terms.

1. Don't compare your routine to others.

Once you begin creating your routine, focus on what you need and try to avoid copying someone else's routine. Inspiration can be helpful at times, but it can send you on the wrong path if you feel pressured to re-create a routine just because you've seen your neighbor, friend, or favorite social media influencer doing it. You may see people posting about the latest diet they're on, running every morning, or joining a weekly mom's club, but that may not work for you. You can see this and instantly believe you need to change what you're currently doing. Instead I recommend thinking about what is of value to you in your life right now and build a routine to support bringing your value to life. Remember, sometimes the lifestyles people portray on social media are only a snapshot, not a daily reality. Stick to what's real to you and ignore the rest.

2. Self-care doesn't have to be alone.

It is a huge myth that you must tackle self-care on your own. If you are called to build a self-care routine that involves your children because you enjoy the bonding or you still want to be able to shower yourself in the company of your significant other, you can do so. This can look like running while pushing a jogging stroller or cooking with your significant other a few days a week. In some seasons of life, this may be your best option of self-care, and that's okay. If the actions in your self-care routine satisfy your needs, then go for it.

3. Align your actions with how you want to feel.

When it comes to self-care, the outcome of your routine will often be an intangible feeling versus a tangible result. To ensure you are getting the outcome you want from your self-care routine, it's helpful to select actions that create the feeling you want to experience. For example, if you are creating a morning routine and your chosen outcome is to feel calm and relaxed, your routine may consist of stretching, meditation, or listening to calming music.

Q: What are some routines I can start that will help me care for myself?

A: There is a range of self-care routines that you can build. The most common include morning, evening, bedtime, exercise and skin care routines. Also remember that you make the rules for your routines and if you want to create a self-care routine you've never heard of, you can do so. Personally, I have a rest routine that supports me in slowing down throughout the day. Below are a few uncommon routines that can help to inspire you to get creative with how you view and indulge in self-care.

⇨ Rest Routine

Suggested steps: Sit down > Close eyes > Deep-breathing exercise

Frequency: After each work day

Timing: ~ 10 minutes

Purpose: To de-stress after the work day

⇨ Hair-Care Routine

Suggested steps: Detangle hair > Wash hair > Deep condition hair > Style

Frequency: Weekly

Timing: ~ 2 hours

Purpose: Stay on top of hair maintenance to promote health and growth

⇨ Meditation Routine

Suggested steps: Light candle > Get in comfortable position > Meditate

Frequency: At night before bed

Timing: ~ 15 minutes

Purpose: To calm the mind before sleep

⇨ Manifestation Routine

Suggested steps: Burn sage > Gratitude practice > Write down current goals you will achieve

Frequency: Weekly

Timing: ~ 15 minutes

Purpose: To make intentional progress in life

⇨ Midday Check-In Routine

Suggested steps: Review daily plan > State your intention for the rest of the day

Frequency: On weekdays (at noon)

Timing: ~ 10 minutes

Purpose: To stay focused throughout the day

⇨ After-Work Routine

Suggested steps: Change into comfy clothes > Turn on playlist > Make dinner

Frequency: Daily after work

Timing: ~ 1.5 hours

Purpose: To know what to expect after the workday

⇨ Spiritual Study Routine

Suggested steps: Choose scripture reading > Read scripture > Journal about reading

Frequency: Each morning

Timing: ~ 25 minutes

Purpose: To consistently connect to your spirituality/source

Q: I manage so many routines on my own. What can help me avoid burnout?

A: Part of self-care is understanding when you need help. Managing multiple routines on your own can become challenging and overwhelming. If you are headed toward burnout or already experiencing the overwhelm of managing it all, there are a few things you can do to lighten your load.

- **Ask for and accept help.** We can't do it all, and it's not beneficial to try. Delegate and ask for help where and when you need it. It takes a village in motherhood and there are people around you who would love to give you a helping hand. Think about who these people are in your life and reach out for assistance. If you struggle with asking for help, it takes practice. You can start by accepting help when someone offers it and gradually begin to ask for small favors, such as help with dinner ideas, best tips for getting your child to sleep better, or to hold you accountable to your routine. Overall, help is vital for maintaining a vibrant life.

- **Decrease your routines.** It may be possible that you have too many routines to manage. Assess your routines and decide which are completely necessary and which can go. To decide which routines to keep, simply ask yourself which ones are best supporting this season of your life. This will instantly lighten your load and create more freedom for you. There's no need to have a million routines, and honestly, that wouldn't be healthy. Make a choice about what stays and what goes.

- **Use tools that support you.** There may be a chance that you don't have much support and asking for help isn't an option. If this is true for you, you can also use tools to manage the routines you have. For some routines, you don't have to be solely responsible for carrying it out; instead you can outsource certain actions. A prime example is hiring a cleaning company to clean your home weekly so you don't have to. This eliminates the need for you to do it yourself and gives you back time to rest or focus on a different priority. Brainstorm where you can outsource parts of your routines.

This will take one if not a few things off your plate and allow you to manage your routines better.

Q: How do I find time for what I need to do and want to do in my day?

A: First, prioritize what you need to do. Needs are subjective and will vary depending on your lifestyle and personality. What I consider as a need may be different from what you see as a need. Decide what is actually needed in your day and plan to address the other needs on a different day. Try not to overload your day with a bunch of needs because there will not be room for your wants. Once you determine what you want to do in your day, schedule it out. Make your wants as nonnegotiable as your needs. There's definitely room in your day to prioritize your needs and wants; it just takes clarity, dispersing your needs appropriately throughout your week, and recognizing that your wants are just as important as your needs. See the example below.

Today's To-Do List

Wants:

- Take a bath (p.m. after child goes to bed)
- Buy skin care products (on lunch break at work)

Needs:

- Work (9 to 5)
- Cook (p.m., order takeout)
- Clean kitchen (p.m., after dinner)
- Wash daughter's hair (p.m., after work during bath)

You'll notice there's not a lot on this to-do list and that there's space for it all. Whenever you find there's not enough time to accomplish your wants and needs, carry them over to the next day and make them priority.

Q: There's always something to do. Will routines help to promote rest?

A: Yes they can, but only if you view and use routines appropriately. Routines should support your life, not consume it. Avoid building routines for every part of your day because this will feed your need to spring into action. When used appropriately, routines will open up more space for rest and give you more opportunity to remain in the present moment. For example, you may be tempted to start the laundry because you finished your previous routine earlier than expected, but since you know your laundry routine will be done tomorrow, you can relax and spend this time incorporating rest into your day.

Q: I'm routined out. Is it ever okay to take a break from my routine?

A: Yes, it is absolutely okay to take a break from your routine with the understanding that your day may look and feel different. A small break from your routine can add some spontaneity to your day; plus, you'll begin to notice the positive difference your routine makes in your life, which can become a strong motivating factor to start again. In addition, wanting to take a break from your routine may also be a sign that your routine may need to be re-created or revamped. However, if your purpose is to have a quick breather, try not to stay away from your routine too long, especially if you want to ease back into the swing of things. Do what feels right for you. If this means putting your routine on hold, do so.

Problem: Jenn was a newly single mom of two kids juggling being a student and facilitating distance learning for her kids. Her life at the time felt out of control and she was doing the best she could to stay above water. She was in need of a predictable schedule and routines to bring order to the chaos.

What helped: Jenn attended my Rock Your Routine Workshop, where the attendees participated in a value identification activity and were taught how to create routines step by step. The values activity was intended to identify what meant the most to each attendee and help them build routines to support their values. This was a huge eye-opener for Jenn.

Outcome: Jenn started a routine to help with keeping her value of self-care front and center. She set self-honoring boundaries around the most important routines, and she no longer feels like she's surviving the day. Through role modeling, her kids have even started routines of their own. Her home is now a haven for herself and her kids.

"When I decided to sign up for Ashley's Rock your Routine Workshop, I had reached a place of desperateness for some sense of normality and predictability. My life felt so out of control! I was a newly single mom caring for my two kids, a full-time graduate student, and the pandemic had me home facilitating distance learning with my kids. Self-care

was nearly non-existent and I felt like I was treading water constantly. I was running myself into the ground and knew something needed to change. After walking through action steps to create routines, I was equipped with the necessary skills to make adjustments that can ebb and flow with life's ever-changing rhythms. I have more peace today than I have had in a very long time. I have set boundaries around my most important routines to protect what matters most to me. My self-care has improved tremendously and we are no longer living life as if we are in a constant state of emergency. My kids know what to expect and have even created some routines of their own! Routines have helped me create the haven in our home that I longed for."

CONCLUSION

Routines are far more than a systematic way to get organized and tame the chaos of life. If created with intention and a healthy perspective, they are fun and flexible tools that create freedom, ease, and happiness. They are your safety harness when life takes unexpected twists and turns. Use routines to your advantage and build them for your unique life. There is no wrong way to create routines. You make the rules, so let your intuition and curiosity guide you.

It is my hope that you received much insight and inspiration from this book and that you return to these pages when you're feeling lost or looking for a source of encouragement to validate you're on the right track. If you remember nothing else from this book, remember that routines don't fit into a box and are built to support your life so you can thrive day to day. There's no pressure to get it right the first time. Have patience with the process and yourself, and allow routines to impact your life in ways beyond your imagination.

Wishing you all the best as you start and continue this journey. Here's to staying happy!

RESOURCES

Routine and Things website (routineandthings.com) is your one-stop shop for all things routine, including products and resources to start, maintain, and enjoy your routines.

Routine and Things podcast (routineandthings.com/blogs/podcast) is a great resource to learn and grow using routine.

Free Routine Assessment (routineandthings.com) can help you figure out which routine you need most right now.

ACKNOWLEDGMENTS

To my supportive partner, incredible daughters, and generous best friend, who each helped to cultivate positivity, joy, and love as I wrote this book. I am forever grateful. To the amazing women who shared a glimpse of your routine-building success with the hope to propel other women forward, thanks for sharing your story. To our growing community of women and mothers who are in search of ease and enjoyment in life, this book is for you. May it open your eyes to the power of routine and allow you to step into your own unique power more and more, day after day.

ABOUT THE AUTHOR

Ashley Brown is an educator, mom of two, and entrepreneur. She is the founder and owner of Routine and Things, a product-based business that equips women to consistently live their happiest life—one routine at a time. She strongly believes routines are a form of wellness and can be a beautiful springboard for improving your home, yourself, and your life.

Ashley holds an MS in nursing from the University of Maryland, Baltimore. She currently resides in Baltimore, Maryland, with her family. She's on a mission to see as many women as possible live life with ease and joy by starting, maintaining, and enjoying routines. Find more inspiration from Ashley at routineandthings.com.